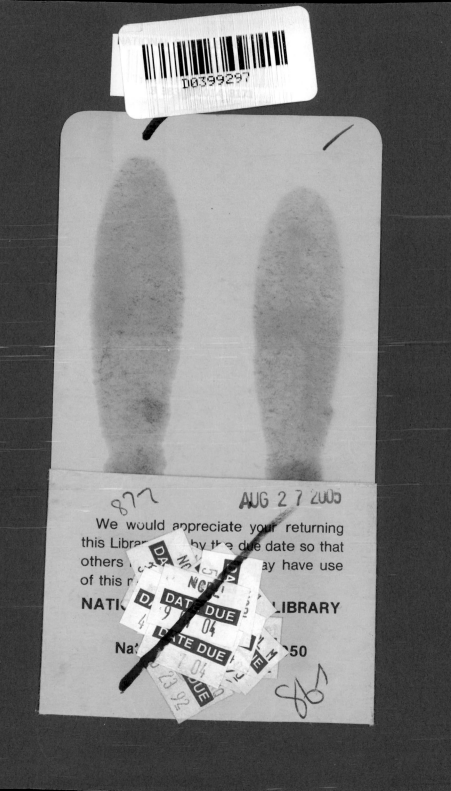

# COMING
## TO
# AMERICA

# Immigrants from the FAR EAST

## LINDA PERRIN

DELACORTE PRESS / NEW YORK

Published by
Delacorte Press
1 Dag Hammarskjold Plaza
New York, N.Y. 10017

Manufactured in the United States of America
First printing

*Picture research by Anne Phalon*

*Designed by Rhea Braunstein*

LIBRARY OF CONGRESS CATALOGING IN PUBLICATION DATA

Perrin, Linda.
    Coming to America.

    Bibliography:  p.
    Includes index.
    SUMMARY:  Discusses the experiences of immigrants
from China, Japan, the Philippines, and Vietnam to the
United States. Includes a chronology of U.S. immigration
laws.
    1.  Asian Americans—History—Juvenile literature.
2.  United States—Race relations—Juvenile literature.
[1.  Asian Americans—History.   2.   United States—
Emigration and immigration.   3.   Race relations]
I. Title.
E184.O6P37        973'.0495          80-65840
ISBN 0-440-01072-1

# Contents

**FROM VIETNAM**

# Introduction

"We are a country of refugees. . . . The United States has always been a nation with an open heart and open arms to receive those people seeking religious freedom and a better way of life." So said President Jimmy Carter when, at a meeting in 1979, he was asked about the wisdom of allowing over 200,000 Vietnamese refugees to come to America.

The President's words express a belief millions of Americans hold: that America has always welcomed the poor and oppressed from around the world. But this is not so. There was no warm welcome for the Irish who fled the potato famine of the 1840s. Labor unions tried to drive out the Italians who came in the early twentieth century. Hungarians, Poles, Greeks, Mexicans—in fact, most immigrant groups —have faced some hostility from native-born Americans. But no other group suffered the kind of treatment dealt to people who came here from the Far

East during the late nineteenth and early twentieth centuries.

The largest of the continents, Asia extends over more than seventeen million square miles. From Japan in the east to the Ural Mountains in the west, from Soviet Central Asia in the north to Indonesia in the south, Asia takes in a multitude of ethnic groups, races, and nations. And from all over this vast area, people have come to America as immigrants. Today, we have fellow citizens who can trace their origins back to such places as China, Japan, Tibet, Korea, India, the Philippines, and Vietnam.

Asia also includes part of the area known as the Middle East, which may be described as stretching from Morocco to Afghanistan. Immigrants from the Middle East will be discussed in a separate book.

Immigration from the Far East began in 1849 when the news reached China that gold had been discovered in California. Chinese men, excited at the prospect of making quick and easy fortunes, began to cross the Pacific. In the decades that followed, other Asians joined them, lured by promises of steady work and high wages.

The majority came to California, which was emerging in the late nineteenth century as a major agricultural and industrial state. Employers, desperate for manpower, looked upon their new Asian employees as a godsend. They found them hard-working, reliable, and willing to take on the most menial of jobs. White workers, however, viewed them less favorably. They resented the employers' preference for Asian workers, and accused the Asians of accepting lower wages than white workers demanded and of taking jobs away from Americans. So while American employers were sending to Asia for more workers, labor unions were calling for a ban on immigration from Asia.

The idea of excluding the Asians found favor in many quarters. The early Asian immigrants on the West Coast came at the same time that millions of immigrants from Europe arrived on the East Coast. Americans began to feel that too many foreigners were coming in, and that something should be done to stop the influx. But whereas most white Europeans could easily blend in with the population, Asians could not. Their physical appearance marked them as foreigners and, as a result, they suffered most from this general, antiforeigner sentiment.

There was also another, more sinister, reason why people protested the presence of Asians in America. White racists held the view that Asians, like American blacks and Indians, were racially inferior. They said people of color were immoral, ignorant savages, incapable of assimilation. These racists vigorously joined the campaign to exclude Asians from the United States.

Under the combined assault of racists, labor unions, and antiforeigner groups, Asians underwent years of harassment and discrimination. Laws were enacted against them; they were unable to become American citizens; they were despised, tormented, beaten. And eventually, America did close her doors to immigrants from Asia—the first time that any ethnic group had been excluded.

It was not until after World War II, during which China and the Philippines fought on the side of the Allies, and Japanese-Americans demonstrated remarkable loyalty to the United States, that attitudes began to change. But there is a long way to go. Present-day immigrants from Asia still find many opportunities closed to them. They still have problems getting jobs and decent housing.

The majority of Asian immigrants came from China, Japan, and the Philippines. The experience of these groups is the subject of this book—along with that of the Vietnamese, whose recent troubled flight from their homeland makes them a special case. For the most part, the story is told by the immigrants themselves. From the diaries they kept, the letters they sent, the books they wrote, and from reports, interviews, and tape recordings, we can gain a vivid insight into the experiences of Asians in America since the days of the gold rush.

# FROM CHINA

# Chapter 1

# The Fortune Seekers

California in 1849 was in an uproar. The greatest gold rush in history had started. Across land and sea came the fortune seekers, changing a quiet, underpopulated area of some 10,000 people into a booming and bustling territory. Over 80,000 people arrived in 1849 alone, and by 1852 California's population had soared to over 250,000.

The number of Chinese who joined the throngs was relatively small. Only about 25,000 had reached California by 1852, yet from the very beginning they attracted attention. With their yellow-brown skins, long black queues, and distinctive features, they were an object of curiosity, for most white men had never seen an Oriental before. One old miner recalled his first glimpse of some Chinese laborers:

> The fellers had made a rush to a spot behind an old Mexican cookin' ranch, and had filled in all around it so tight that it was fifteen minutes

3

before I come to a view of the cause o' their muss. Some of the chaps hollered, "A ring! A ring!" and when they began to spread out, there in the middle, lookin' mightly skeered, was a lot o' fellers with long tails to their heads and short trousers, besides great broadbrimmed wooden hats and a pole like a neck yoke over each shoulder. They were queer-lookin' chicks, and no mistake. The chaps around made a big ring and yelled and hooted, and finally began to throw things at 'em to git 'em mad, but old Dick Losha stepped in front on 'em, and with the revolvers in his hands, said, "Look o' here, fellers, these 'ere chaps haint done no harm and don't know our talk, so yer see we don't want ter abuse 'em. They've been sent up here to work, and there's more a-comin'. We can hire 'em cheap when we want 'em, so let 'em stay. They're better nor the cussed Injun anyhow." All the fellers said, "All right, old boy, let 'em come."[1]

It didn't take long for employers to realize that, not only were the Chinese better than the "cussed Injun," they were better than most other workers. Honest, hardworking, and reliable, and not too proud to take on jobs that other men shunned, the Chinese were soon in great demand. And when the gold rush was over a few years later, there were other activities that required their services.

California was emerging as a major agricultural

and industrial state. Chinese laborers helped build the railroads; they worked in factories and mills; they reclaimed swamplands; they were gardeners and domestic servants. Some established their own businesses. In the thirty years following the gold rush, more than a quarter million Chinese came across the Pacific to take advantage of the California economic boom.

Most of the early Chinese immigrants were poor, uneducated peasants, forced to go abroad by conditions in China. For centuries the peasants in China had lived in the country, scratching out a living from the soil. Life was always a struggle. Only by working together as a unit, with men, women, and children toiling in the fields, could a family hope to survive. The responsibility of managing the family's activities rested with the head of the household, usually the father. He saw to it that the work was done, that children were raised to respect their elders, that family graveyards were maintained and that aging parents were looked after. Under normal circumstances he would never have considered leaving home.

But circumstances were not normal in the mid-nineteenth century. China was in turmoil. The ruling Manchus had allowed power to fall into the hands of corrupt officials who were demanding ever higher taxes from the peasants. The officials took little interest in the affairs of their local communities, so when disputes between villages arose, fighting often broke out. At the same time, secret societies, intent on gaining control of the countryside, and of overthrowing the corrupt officials, fought pitched battles during which entire villages were destroyed.

Meanwhile, China was also under pressure from outside. For centuries it had been a closed society, isolated from the rest of the world. Foreigners were not welcome and most attempts by Western countries to trade with China had been firmly repulsed. Only the port of Canton was open to foreigners, and their activities were closely regulated. Western countries resented the restrictions. By the 1830s the Industrial Revolution in Europe was under way and companies wanted to sell their goods in the vast China market and to obtain raw materials.

The Opium War of 1839–42 presented them with the opportunity they sought. Britain invaded China after a Chinese official confiscated and destroyed a large consignment of opium, the sale of which was banned in China. The British defeated the emperor's army and demanded that China open up more ports to foreign trade. Many Chinese resented the foreign "invasion," seeing it as a threat to their traditional way of life. In the years that followed they showed their resentment by staging numerous revolts.

Peasant communities suffered enormously during this turbulent period. Many people lost their homes and land in the fighting; others, unable to pay their taxes, were thrown off their land. Adding to the misery, severe droughts in the late 1840s caused great crop failures.

In these circumstances, it is not surprising that

when news of the California gold strike reached
China, there were men ready to pull up stakes and go
prospecting. Nor is it surprising that thousands more
jumped at the opportunity of other types of employment in California during the years following the
gold rush. Most of them felt that there was no
alternative. If they were to support their families, as
tradition demanded, they had to go abroad. Besides,
it would only be for a few years. They would work
hard, earn plenty of money, return to China, and live
the rest of their lives in comfort.

With that belief to sustain them, they said goodbye to their families and set off for Hong Kong, the
main port of departure. There, ship captains and
recruitment agents, armed with misleading circulars,
awaited them, ready to reassure the unwary or un-
decided. An American clergyman who was in China
during the mid-nineteenth century came across this
advertisement:

> Americans are very rich people. They want the
> Chinaman to come and will make him very
> welcome. There you will have great pay, large
> houses, and food and clothing of the finest
> description. You can write to your friends and
> send them money at any time, and we will be
> responsible for the safe delivery. . . . There are
> a great many Chinamen there now, and it will
> not be a strange country. China god is there,
> and the agents of this house. Never fear and
> you will be lucky. Come to Hong Kong, or to

the sign of this house in Canton, and we will instruct you. Money is in great plenty and to spare in America.[2]

Advertisements like this persuaded thousands of Chinese to go off to America in search of the promised riches. But their hopes were mixed with fear and apprehension. The Western way of life was different from the Chinese, and the tales circulating about Western morals and manners were discouraging. Lee Chew, a farmer's son who immigrated to America and was interviewed about the story of his life, describes what he was taught about the Western foreigners:

> I heard much concerning the red haired, green eyed foreign devils with the hairy faces, who had lately come out of the sea and clustered on our shores. They were wild and fierce and wicked. . . . They loved to beat people and to rob and murder. In the streets of Hong Kong many of them could be seen reeling drunk. Their speech was a savage roar, like the voice of the tiger or the buffalo. . . . Their men and women lived together like animals, without any marriage or faithfulness, and even were shameless enough to walk the streets arm in arm in daylight.[3]

Despite their misgivings many Chinese also had an intense curiosity about the foreigners. While utterly convinced that China was superior in all things, they had to acknowledge that some foreign inventions were truly amazing. Explained Lee Chew:

My grandfather said that it was well known that the Chinese were always the greatest and wisest among men. They had invented and discovered everything that was good. Therefore the things which the foreign devils had and the Chinese had not must be evil. Some of these things were very wonderful, enabling the red haired savages to talk with one another, though they might be thousands of miles apart [the telegraph]. They had suns that made darkness like day, their ships carried earthquakes and volcanoes to fight for them, and thousands of demons that lived in iron and steel houses spun their cotton and silk, pushed their boats, pulled their cars, printed their newspapers and did other work for them.[4]

Curious but apprehensive about such inventions, many Chinese wondered if they dared risk an encounter with the "foreign devils." But then, during the late 1850s, some of the first Chinese to go to America began to return home. That they came back at all was reassuring. That they came laden with riches even more so. Lee Chew recalled the triumphant return of one of his neighbors:

[When] I was about sixteen years of age, a man of our tribe came back from America and took ground as large as four city blocks and made a paradise of it. He put a large stone wall around and led some streams through and built a palace and summer house and about twenty other structures. . . .

The man had gone away from our village a poor boy. Now he returned with unlimited wealth, which he had obtained in the country of the American wizards.[5]

Once the man had finished building his palace, he held a party for the people in the village:

One hundred pigs roasted whole were served on the tables, with chickens, ducks, geese and such an abundance of dainties that our villagers even now lick their fingers when they think of it. He had the best actors from Hong Kong performing, and every musician for miles around was playing and singing.

Having made his wealth among the barbarians this man had faithfully returned to pour it out among his tribesmen, and he is living in our village now very happy, and a pillar of strength to the poor.[6]

What an inducement such a display of wealth must have been to the other villagers. If he could do it, why couldn't they? But deciding to emigrate was only the beginning. The next step was to find a way of getting to America—and that wasn't easy.

# Chapter 2

# En Route to the Golden Mountain

The fare for the Pacific crossing in the mid-nineteenth century was about forty dollars—a small fortune to the ordinary Chinese peasant, whose yearly earnings amounted to twenty or thirty dollars at the most. Few could raise the necessary sum, or the extra money needed to bribe Chinese officials, for emigration from China was illegal.

Most Chinese, therefore, had to enter into debt to get ticket money. One way they could do this was through the contract labor system. The hopeful emigrant borrowed the ticket money from an employer in America and agreed to work for a specified period of time, during which he would receive little or no money. Many emigrants were swindled. Dishonest employers took advantage of their inability to read or write, and had them sign contracts committing them to work far beyond the years they thought they had agreed to.

Another way out was the credit-ticket system,

under which most Chinese came to America. Chinese merchants or agents already in San Francisco, working through brokers in Hong Kong, lent the ticket money to the emigrant and he was obliged to pay it back within a fixed time limit. This system, too, was open to abuse. Some emigrants ended up paying more than one hundred dollars for tickets, for high interest rates and brokers' fees were added.

The ocean crossing generally took from four to six weeks. For the Chinese emigrants, packed like sardines in the bowels of the ship, it was a miserable time. Lee Chew, the farmer's son, recalled his passage:

> I went to Hong Kong with five other boys and we got steerage passage on a steamer, paying $50 each. Everything was new to me. All my life I had been used to sleeping on a board bed with a wooden pillow, and I found the steamer's bunk very uncomfortable because it was so soft. The food was different from that which I had been used to, and I did not like it at all. I was afraid of the stews, for the thought of what they might be made of by the wicked wizards of the ship made me ill.[1]

How did the immigrants feel when their ship finally arrived in San Francisco? Probably relieved that the journey was finally over; apprehensive about what lay ahead in this strange land; and homesick. But overriding all these emotions was hope—they were in "the Golden Mountain," for that is what the

Chinese called California. This was where they would make their fortune.

An American reporter described the scene as a ship docked in San Francisco:

> Her main deck is packed with Chinamen—every foot of space being occupied by them—who are gazing in silent wonder at the new land whose fame has reached them beyond the seas, and whose riches these . . . representatives of the toiling millions of Asia have come to develop. . . .
>
> A living stream of the blue-coated men from Asia, bearing long bamboo poles across their shoulders, from which depend packages of bedding, matting, clothing, and things of which we know neither the names nor the uses, pours down the plank the moment the word is given, "All ready!"[2]

The new immigrants, whom the reporter estimated to be between fifteen and forty years of age, were quickly organized. Waiting for them on the quay were the agents who had arranged their passage and representatives from various Chinese societies.

> As they come down upon the wharf, they separate into messes or gangs of ten, twenty, or thirty each, and being recognized through some, to us, incomprehensible free-masonry systems of signs by the agents . . . are assigned places on the long, broad-shedded wharf which

has been cleared especially for their accommodation and the convenience of the customs officers. . . . For two mortal hours the blue stream pours down from the steamer upon the wharf. You wonder where such a swarm of human beings found stowage room—the bulk already seems greater than that of the steamer.[3]

To help new arrivals, a number of societies had been formed. Clan societies protected related families; district societies looked after men from the same district. An article in the *Overland Monthly* described their activities:

The chief purpose of the [societies] was to assist newcomers. Some of the Chinese, who had never been more than fifty or one hundred miles from their birthplace, were almost unable to take care of themselves when they first arrived here. When a ship arrived at San Francisco from China, the society sent some wagons to bring the newcomers and their baggage up to Chinatown. The society also supplied the newcomers with room, water, and wood, for a month or two, until they could go into the mines or other occupations.[4]

Some form of protection was essential, claimed the writer, given the conditions in California at that time:

The reader must bear in mind the early life of California, when she was almost a "cesspool" for all elements of the world. Fighting and quarreling were the daily amusements of the early Californians. The condition of affairs then was like a boiler overloaded with steam, which seeks for the weakest part of the cylinder to escape. The unfortunate Mongolians [Chinese] were the weakest element. Hence all others pitched into them. Having experienced all these circumstances, and mingled with a people [Americans] whose appearance, language, and customs were unknown to them, the Chinese formed [societies] so that they might protect each other.[5]

Eventually the various societies merged into the Six Companies, one for each of the districts from which most of the immigrants came. The Companies built clubhouses for the men where they could stay when in Chinatown, and generally looked after their welfare. One of their most important functions, in the eyes of the Chinese, was to see to the shipment back to China of the bones of any immigrant who had died, so that he could be honored as tradition demanded.

But the Six Companies were far more than a charitable organization. They were immensely powerful, controlling the destinies of many of the Chinese immigrants. They saw to it that the contract laborers fulfilled the terms of their contracts, and that those immigrants who came on a credit ticket paid back their debts in full. Immigrants who wanted to go back to China before their debts were paid found the way barred, for the Six Companies had an arrangement with the main steamship company whereby no Chinese could get a ticket without a permit from the Companies.

The power of the Six Companies spread to every area where there was a Chinese quarter, but it was always strongest in the San Francisco Chinatown. For it was to that city within a city that most of the Chinese immigrants first made their way, some to move on to other areas, some to stay.

The San Francisco newspaper *Daily Alta* described the Chinatown of the mid-1850s:

> The majority of houses were of Chinese importation, and were stores, stocked with hams, tea, dried fish, dried ducks, and other . . . Chinese eatables, besides copper pots and kettles, fans, shawls, chessmen, and all sorts of curiosities. Suspended over the doors were brilliantly-colored boards . . . covered with Chinese characters . . . while the streets were thronged with . . . Celestials,* chattering vociferously as they rushed about from store to store, or standing in groups studying the Chinese bills posted up in the shop windows, which may have been play-bills—for there was a Chinese theatre—or perhaps advertisements.

Chinatown was a home away from home. Chinese men who worked in San Francisco—in the cigar factories, shoe factories, woolen mills, and other in-

---

* China was known as the Celestial Empire and the Chinese as Celestials.

dustries—could return there in the evenings and relax after long hours on the job. They would be joined, at weekends and holidays, by Chinese men from the mining camps, railroads and farms, to whom Chinatown was a refuge. There they could find familiar food, speak their own language, indulge their love of gambling, and take part in traditional Chinese celebrations.

But behind its colorful facade there was a seamier side of life to Chinatown. It was overcrowded. Many of its residents were poor, for in addition to paying off their debts they were also sending money home to support their families. And there were few women, since only a handful of the immigrants could afford to bring their wives with them. What women there were were often prostitutes, known as singsong girls.

And then there were the tongs, criminal organizations which were largely responsible for the reputation that Chinatown gained among Americans as a place of dark intrigue, sinister crime, and dens of iniquity. The tongs challenged the Six Companies for control of Chinatown. They were unsuccessful, but they did gain control of vice—prostitution, gambling, and opium.

[The tongs ruled by terror, demanding protection money from establishments throughout Chinatown.] Their victims were too terrified to testify against them, for the activities of their "highbinders"—men who killed on contract—were well known. A former prostitute, Chun Ho, described one episode she had witnessed:

I saw one [prostitute] after she had been killed by a highbinder. This highbinder wanted money from her; she either did not have it or put him off, but because she did not pay the money he wanted she was shot by him. . . . I also know of three other women that have been killed by highbinders. Two of these were shot and one stabbed to death. As a rule, the murderers of girls forced to lead that life are never brought to justice, because no one would dare to testify against the murderers.[6]

Nearly all the singsong girls were slaves. Some had been kidnapped, but many had been sold by their own families. The selling of children was not uncommon in China, and in fact the government sanctioned it. Needy families had, for generations, sold their children into domestic slavery. The sale of daughters into prostitution was merely an extension of this practice. Chun Ho, for instance, was sold by her mother for two hundred dollars. She explained how it happened:

When I was nineteen years old, the mistress No. 3 of a noted procurer by the name of Gwan Lung, who lives in San Francisco, went back to Canton, where my mother happened to be living with me at that time, and gave me glowing accounts of life in California. She painted that life so beautifully that I was seized with an inclination to go there and try my fortune, mother taking $200 and consenting to my going.[7]

Once in California, the singsong girls were controlled by pimps or madams, who paid extortion money to the tongs. Virtual prisoners, the girls were at the mercy of the tongs, and were frequently beaten or tortured. Chun Ho spoke of her ordeal:

> My owners were never satisfied, no matter how much money I made. When they were angered in any way, they would vent their anger upon me, which they would also do upon the other girls. . . . They very often removed us from the houses of ill-repute to family dwellings when they wanted to punish us, so that anyone passing by could not hear our cries very well. . . . The instruments used were wooden clubs and sometimes anything they could lay their hands on; and one time I was threatened with a pistol held at me. The work of removing myself and the other girls from where we were to family places where we were punished was done by members of the highbinder societies. That was part of their work, for which they receive pay.[8]

Chun Ho eventually managed to escape to a rescue home, one of a number of missions that were established by concerned individuals to provide shelter for the singsong girls and others in need of help. Even in the rescue home, however, she felt far from secure:

> The matron of the Rescue Home came with the police and had me rescued. That was

about a year ago, and I am still in the home, but I understand Tsoy Lung Bo [her owner] has ever since, from time to time, been demanding from me the amount he paid for me, threatening to kill me if I should not pay it before going home to China or leaving the mission. Highbinder after highbinder . . . have been going backward and forward in the vicinity of the home, threatening me and saying it would be much better for me to return to this man; that if I valued life at all to go right back, as the matron of the home could not always protect me. I have an aunt living near the home and sometimes I have visited her, thinking they would not know; but they soon found out, and even threatened my aunt, saying that if she persisted in keeping me, if any harm came to her they would not be responsible.[9]

This, then, was Chinatown in the mid to late nineteenth century—a place where poverty, violence, and vice were commonplace, but also a place that provided a temporary home and shelter for the new immigrants pouring in from China. Some settled there; others moved on. But for all of them it was the beginning of a new life.

# Chapter 3

# The New Life

Most of the first wave of Chinese who came to California considered themselves sojourners—temporary visitors who would make their fortune and then return to China. They did not, therefore, attempt to become "Americanized," but tended to stay in their own groups, which was to cause trouble later on.

At first they were welcomed as industrious, colorful, and quaint. Those Chinese who went to the goldfields did not fight over claims. They preferred to pick over abandoned claims than to risk conflicts with the more aggressive white miners. Many did not even look for gold, for they quickly discovered that there were other ways of making money in California.

California's population in the 1850s was about ninety percent male. The men who came looking for gold generally came alone. They wanted to be free to move from camp to camp as new discoveries were made. A wife and children would have been an encumbrance. But they still needed someone to do the traditional "women's work"—washing, cooking, and cleaning. The Chinese, ready to turn their hand to anything that would earn a living, filled the gap. They set up laundries, opened restaurants, and worked as cooks at the mining camps.

Some Chinese worked as domestic servants in the homes of the lawyers, politicians, doctors, teachers, and others who had followed the gold seekers to California, knowing that there would be a demand for their services. California's rich soil also attracted thousands of land speculators and farmers and they, too, employed Chinese servants. During the last half of the nineteenth century, almost every well-to-do home in California had a staff of Chinese servants.

Domestic work, laundering, and cooking did not come easily to the Chinese. They were no more experienced in this type of work than any other men but, as Lee Chew pointed out, they soon learned:

> A man got me work as a house servant in an American family, and my start was the same as that of almost all the Chinese in this country.
>
> The Chinese laundryman does not learn his trade in China; there are no laundries in China. The women there do the washing in tubs and have no washboards or flat irons. All the Chinese laundrymen here were taught in the first place by American women just as I was taught.

When I went to work for that American
family I could not speak a word of English. . . .
I did not know how to do anything, and I did
not understand what the lady said to me, but
she showed me how to cook, wash, iron, sweep,
dust, make beds, wash dishes, clean windows,
paint and brass, polish the knives and forks.[1]

The laundry business was particularly appealing
to the Chinese because it required little capital to get
started. In later years, when discrimination excluded
the Chinese from many fields of employment,
laundering was one of the few occupations still open
to them. As a result, there were Chinese laundries
in most American cities by the turn of the century.

But for a while, at least, there was plenty of
work for the Chinese. Those who had worked for
the mining companies had proved to be meticulous,
honest and hardworking, so when the California
economy began to expand in new directions, employers turned to the Chinese.

One of the major employers of Chinese labor in
the 1860s was the Central Pacific Railroad. At first
it had been reluctant to take on the Chinese, fearing
that because of their slight stature they would not
be up to the strenuous nature of the job. But the
railroad company was desperate for men, and since
most who made their way to California preferred to
try their luck in the goldfields, the railroad decided
to give the Chinese a try.

The Central Pacific started off with fifty Chinese
laborers, on a trial basis. The *Sacramento Union* of

June 15, 1858, reported that the railroad found them to be "very good working hands."

> They do not work as rapidly as the white men, but they keep constantly at it from sunrise until sunset. The experiment bids fair to demonstrate that Chinese laborers can be profitably employed in grading railroads in California.

And employed they were, in their thousands. The railroad took on every able-bodied Chinese it could find and sent to China for more. Of the ten thousand men who built the Central Pacific, nine thousand were Chinese. Charles Crocker, general superintendent of the Central Pacific, described their performance as "equal to the best white men." He recalled their efforts in digging the tunnel through the Donner Summit:

> The company were in a very great hurry for that tunnel . . . and they urged me to get the very best Cornish miners. . . . We went to Virginia City and got some Cornish miners out of those mines and paid them extra wages. We put them into one side of the shaft . . . and we had Chinamen on the other side. We measured the work every Sunday morning; and the Chinamen without fail always outmeasured the Cornish miners; that is to say, they would cut more rock in a week than the Cornish miners did, and there it was hard work, steady pounding on the rock, bone-labor.[2]

The Chinese also found work on the many farms in California. Here, too, they proved to be diligent and careful workers and soon they were in great demand. A farmer explained:

> We had a very large wheatfield. It was harvest-time, and the superintendent wrote down to send him up a couple of hundred white men. . . . Those men would not work more than two or three days, or a week, and then they would quit. . . . I then went to a Chinaman and told him I wanted to contract for binding and [stacking] wheat. . . . Several hundred of them came. We had one or two hundred acres that had been reaped, and needed putting up very badly; and the next morning it was all [stacked]. The Chinamen did the work that night. They did the work well and faithfully, and of course we abandoned white labor.[3]

But popular though the Chinese were with employers, they were fast losing favor in other quarters. White laborers, resenting the success of the Chinese in getting and keeping jobs, accused them of providing cheap labor and taking jobs away from Americans. Some went so far as to claim that the Chinese were slaves, imported and controlled by the Six Companies. This notion was based in part on the fact that Chinese laborers, or coolies, had been imported as slaves into South America, and in part on the fact that the controlling influence of the Six Companies did, to an outsider, strongly suggest that the Chinese were slaves.

The notion that the Chinese were slaves was profoundly disturbing to Californians. In 1849 they had adopted a state constitution prohibiting slavery, and California had joined the Union one year later as a free, or nonslave, state. Californians wanted to avoid the conflicts over slavery that were dividing the eastern states and that would eventually lead to civil war. The Chinese were, therefore, seen as a constant threat to the stability of California and many people began to call for their expulsion from the state.

The outcry was scarcely justified. The Chinese were not slaves, nor were they taking jobs away from Americans. Indeed, Americans would not have accepted many of the jobs that the Chinese took, considering the work too menial or degrading. No American would have worked as a laundryman, for instance, or as a domestic servant. Moreover, the accusation that the Chinese were accepting low wages, and thus lowering wage levels generally, was rarely true. The majority of Chinese laborers received similar wages to their white counterparts. As Lee Chew put it:

> The cheap labor cry was always a falsehood. [Our] labor was never cheap, and is not cheap now. It has always commanded the highest market price. But the trouble is that the Chinese are such excellent and faithful workers that bosses will have no others when they can get them. If you look at men working on the street you will find an overseer for every four or five of them. That watching is not necessary for

Chinese. They work as well when left to themselves as they do when someone is looking at them.

It was the jealousy of laboring men of other nationalities—especially the Irish—that raised all the outcry against the Chinese. No one would hire an Irishman, German, Englishman or Italian when he could get a Chinese, because our countrymen are so much more honest, industrious, steady, sober and painstaking. Chinese were persecuted, not for their vices, but for their virtues.[4]

But there was far more behind the accusations than jealousy. The arrival of the Chinese coincided with a rise of nativism on the part of older Americans. This had been triggered by the huge influx of more than half a million Irish immigrants during the late 1840s. Driven out of their country by a devastating famine, the Irish poured into New York and Boston. They were poor, weak, and unskilled. And they were Catholics.

The dominant white Anglo-Saxon Protestants bitterly resented the Irish presence in their cities. America, they maintained, was a Protestant country. Catholics, especially poor Catholics, were not welcome. Nor, they decided, were other minority groups. The Irish immigration had led to a new wave of nativism—which was to affect all nonwhite, non-Protestant immigrants. The Chinese in California were an obvious target for hostility.

The combined attack on the Chinese of nativists, white laborers, and antislavery groups was vicious. So numerous, and so powerful, were these pressure groups, that the California legislature was able to pass a series of bills, aimed specifically at the Chinese. They were declared ineligible for citizenship. They were forced to pay higher taxes than anyone else. Since they were not white, they could not testify against whites in court (which meant that they were not protected by the law). They were required to send their children to separate schools (but separate schools were not built). They were not allowed to marry white women.

Rebuffed by white society, the Chinese retreated more and more into their own communities. Soon there were Chinatowns in all the main cities of the West. But incredibly, white society resented this, too, charging that the Chinatowns were an alien presence in the cities where they existed.

Then there were Americans who, objecting to the presence of Chinese men, went to the opposite extreme and complained about the absence of Chinese women. Why did the men not bring their wives from China? The answer, of course, was simple—they couldn't afford to—but the Americans chose to ignore this explanation, and claimed that the Chinese preferred the company of their singsong girls.

It seemed that the Chinese could do nothing right. Everything about them was criticized—even the clothes they wore. But they had good reasons for keeping their traditional costumes as Lee Chew wrote:

Some fault is found with us for sticking to our
old customs here, especially in the matter of
clothes, but the reason is that we find American
clothes much inferior, so far as comfort and
warmth go. The Chinaman's coat for the winter
is very durable, very light and very warm. It
is easy and not in the way. If he wants to work
he slips out of it in a moment and can put it on
again as quickly. Our shoes and hats also are
better, we think, for our purposes, than the
American clothes. Most of us have tried the
American clothes, and they make us feel as if
we were in the stocks.[5]

Wherever the Chinese went, they were mistreated
and harassed. Lee Chew, who, because a laundryman, reported:

We went to a town about 500 miles inland,
where a railroad was being built. . . . We had to
put up with many insults and some frauds, as
men would come in and claim parcels that did
not belong to them, saying they had lost their
tickets, and would fight if they did not get what
they asked for.
Sometimes we were taken before magistrates
and fined for losing shirts that we had never
seen.[6]

Matters proved to be no better when the laundryman
moved to a new location:

We were three years with the railroad, and then
went to the mines where we made plenty of

money in gold dust, but had a hard time, for many of the miners were wild men who carried revolvers and after drinking would come into our place to shoot and steal shirts, for which we had to pay. One of these men hit his head against a flat iron and all the miners came and broke up our laundry, chasing us out of town. They were going to hang us. We lost all our property and $365 in money, which members of the mob must have found.[7]

Rejection, harassment, discrimination—the new life was proving to be far different from what the Chinese immigrants had expected. But worse was to come.

# Chapter 4

# "The Chinese Must Go!"

For more than twenty years after the discovery of gold, California was the great land of opportunity. Nobody, it seemed, could fail to make money there. It had gold and silver; it had rich agricultural land; railroad building and industry provided employment for thousands. Over half a million people had moved there by 1870, all of them determined to share in California's prosperity.

Suddenly the dream was shattered. In 1873 the United States entered a period of economic depression. The enormous cost of the Civil War, combined with excessive railroad building, losses from wild commercial ventures, overconfidence, inflated credit, and the investment of too much capital in new land led to the failure of the stock market. The boom days were over. During the next five years railroad building almost stopped, industrial development came to a standstill, and many businesses failed. In

31

California, as elsewhere, thousands of people were thrown out of work.

At the same time, immigrants were continuing to come to America. Many people began to resent this, saying there were not enough jobs to go around, and foreigners should be kept out of the country. No group was more "foreign" than the Chinese. Though vastly outnumbered by German, Irish, and Scandinavian immigrants, the Chinese were so much more visible than the Europeans that they bore the brunt of the campaigns against foreigners.

Throughout the depression years, unemployed workers complained that the Chinese were taking jobs away from white men. A popular song, published in 1877, put the thought to music.

## TWELVE HUNDRED MORE[1]

O workingmen dear, and did you hear
The news that's goin' round?
Another China steamer
Has been landed here in town.
Today I read the papers,
And it grieved my heart full sore
To see upon the title page,
O, just "Twelve Hundred More!"

O, California's coming down,
As you can plainly see.
They are hiring all the Chinamen
and discharging you and me;
But strife will be in every town
Throughout the Pacific shore,

And the cry of old and young shall be,
"O, damn, 'Twelve Hundred More.' "

They run their steamer in at night
Upon our lovely bay;
If 'twas a free and honest trade,
They'd land it in the day.
They come here by the hundreds—
The country is overrun—
And go to work at any price—
By them the labor's done.

If you meet a workman in the street
And look into his face,
You'll see the signs of sorrow there—
Oh, damn this long-tailed race!
And men today are languishing
Upon a prison floor,
Because they've been supplanted by
This vile "Twelve Hundred More!"

Twelve hundred honest laboring men
Thrown out of work today
By the landing of these Chinamen
In San Francisco Bay.
Twelve hundred pure and virtuous girls,
In the papers I have read,
Must barter away their virtue
To get a crust of bread.

This state of things can never last
In this, our golden land,
For soon you'll hear the avenging cry,
"Drive out the China man!"

And then we'll have the stirring times
We had in days of yore,
And the devil take those dirty words
They call "Twelve Hundred More!"

But there was more to the anti-Chinese movement
than that jobs were hard to find. The nativist view,
that America should remain a white, Protestant
country, had found widespread support by now.
Many whites considered the Chinese to be racially
inferior and incapable of assimilation. An 1877
report by the California Senate summarized nativist
objections to the Chinese as follows:

> During their entire settlement in California,
> they have never adapted themselves to our
> habits, mode of dress, or our educational sys-
> tem, have never learned the sanctity of an oath,
> never desired to become citizens, or to perform
> the duties of citizenship, never discovered the
> difference between right and wrong, never
> ceased the worship of their idol gods, or ad-
> vanced a step beyond the traditions of their
> native hive. Impregnable to all the influences
> of our Anglo-Saxon life, they remain the same
> stolid Asiatics that have floated on the rivers
> and slaved in the fields of China for thirty
> centuries of time. . . .
>     Of all the vast horde not four hundred have
> been brought to a realization of the truths of
> Christianity. . . . It is safe to say that where one
> Chinese soul has been saved . . . a hundred

white have been lost by the contamination of their presence.[2]

Some criticism of the Chinese was, perhaps, justified. After all, few of them made any attempt to adapt themselves to the American way of life. Most were concerned only with making money and then returning home to China. But the criticism of them went far beyond this. Racists accused them of countless "sins" for which there was no justification, and referred to them as the "yellow peril." Robert Louis Stevenson, the writer, who was in San Francisco during the depression years, commented on some of the accusations:

> The Chinese are considered stupid, because they are imperfectly acquainted with English. They are held to be base, because their dexterity and frugality enable them to underbid the lazy, luxurious Caucasian. They are said to be thieves; I am sure they have no monopoly on that. They are called cruel; the Anglo-Saxon and the cheerful Irishman may each reflect before he bears the accusation.[3]

But Stevenson's eloquent defense of the Chinese had little effect. The anti-Chinese feeling was too strong to be contained. Further discriminatory measures were passed by the California legislature. There was the famous Queue Ordinance of 1873, for instance, which stated that Chinese prisoners must have their queues, or braids, cut off. For a

Chinese man this was a great indignity. The tradition of wearing a queue dated back to the mid-seventeenth century and Chinese men were proud of their braids. Another ordinance, forbidding the removal of bodies or bones without the coroner's permission, was directed against the Chinese tradition of sending the bones of the dead back to China for burial. This practice was important to the Chinese who believed that, by transferring the bones of a dead man to China, they were also sending his spirit back home.

One of the most vociferous spokesmen for white workers opposed to the Chinese in California was Dennis Kearney. Kearney, an immigrant from Ireland, was the founder of the Workingmen's Party, a powerful labor union. He was a spellbinding orator and he rallied the white workers with the slogan "The Chinese Must Go!" At nightly meetings in San Francisco he would urge his followers to rid themselves of the "filthy coolies." This account of one of his meetings appeared in a San Francisco newspaper in 1876:

## A RIOTOUS ASSEMBLY

An inflammatory/ Anti-Chinese Meeting was held last evening on Kearney Street, and addressed by an incendiary orator./ Under his heated harangue, the crowd was wrought up to the highest pitch of excitement, and increased in numbers until the street was blocked by a surging mass. The speaker read a long series of resolutions condemning the importation of coolies, demanding a remedy from the law-making power, and ended by proclaiming that if no measures were taken to suppress the plague, the people were justified in taking summary vengeance on the Mongolians. The resolutions were received with yells by the listeners, and several unlucky Chinamen who passed by at the moment were knocked down and kicked, to emphasize the verdict. The speaker then resumed his address in a more incendiary strain than before, calling on the populace, in the name of humanity, and their families, and as American citizens, to "drive every greasy-faced coolie from the land." "We must take this insidious monster by the throat," shouted the speaker, "and throttle it until its heart ceases to beat, and then hurl it into the sea!" At the conclusion of this speech he called upon every man to sign the resolutions, which about two hundred of those present did. During the crowding up to accomplish this, a car passed along on which a Chinaman was riding. Yells of "pull him off! Lynch him! Kill the greasy slave!" etc. rent the air; but the Mongolian escaped with only a few cuffs and a vigorous kick or two. . . . [4]

Anti-Chinese riots erupted in San Francisco, in Los Angeles, and in mining towns throughout California. In July 1877 angry mobs set fire to twenty-five Chinese laundries in San Francisco. In November 1878 the whole Chinese population of

Truckee, California, which numbered about one thousand, was driven out of town. Gangs of rioters robbed and destroyed Chinese homes. White workers threatened employers of Chinese labor with violence unless they dismissed their Chinese workers. Signboards stating No Chinese Need Apply became a common sight. Hotels, restaurants, and barbershops refused to serve Chinese customers.

Assaults on the Chinese became so common that they were warned to stay off the streets. The same newspaper reported:

> It is scarcely safe for a Chinaman to walk the streets in certain parts of this city. When seen, whether by day or night, they are mercilessly pelted with stones by the young scape-graces who now, there being no school, have nothing else to do, while older hoodlums look on approvingly, and, if the Chinamen venture to resist the assaults, take a hand in and assist the youngsters. Chinese wash houses are sacked almost nightly. A Chinaman apparently has no rights which a white hoodlum, big or little, is bound to respect.[5]

In a series of letters, Kwang Chang Ling, a Chinese leader, tried to defend his fellow countrymen. In one letter he argued that California could not afford to lose its Chinese labor force:

> The cry is here that the Chinese must go. I say they should not go; that they cannot go; that they will not go. More than this, that, were it

conceivable that they went, your State would be ruined; in a word that the Chinese population of the Pacific Coast have become indispensable to its continued prosperity, and that you cannot afford to part with them.[6]

Another letter pointed to a "glaring contradiction" in American attitudes:

Let me . . . endeavor to correct one great misapprehension in respect to the Chinaman. You are continually objecting to his morality. Your travelers say he is depraved; your missionaries call him ungodly; your commissioners call him uncleanly. . . . Yet your housewives permit him to wait upon them at table; they admit him to their bed-chambers; they confide to him their garments and jewels; and even trust their lives to him, by awarding him supreme control over their kitchens and the preparation of their food.[7]

And on the question of religion:

Is it the religion of the Chinese residents in America of which you complain? What right have you to do this, with freedom of religion guaranteed in your Federal and State constitutions and a hundred monstrous sects flourishing in your midst and protected by your laws? There are more Shakers than Buddhists, more Mormons than Confucians, in your country; and, while the latter keep their religion to

themselves, the former flaunt theirs, with all
its repulsive features, in the face of your moral
code, which it flatly insults.[8]

Rational arguments were ignored. The anti-
Chinese riots continued unabated and eventually
the rioters achieved their aim. In 1882, under pressure from powerful labor unions, most notably
Dennis Kearney's Workingmen's Party, Congress
decided that the mass immigration from China
must end, and it passed the first Chinese Exclusion
Act. The act allowed Chinese diplomats, students,
and merchants to enter the United States as usual,
but ordinary workers were to be excluded for ten
years. This was the first time that America had
closed her doors to people from any country.

The Chinese were stunned. What had they done to
deserve such treatment? In their view, as expressed
here by Lee Chew, they were far more acceptable
than certain other national groups:

> Irish fill the almshouses and prisons and orphan
> asylums, Italians are among the most dangerous
> of men, Jews are unclean and ignorant. Yet
> they are all let in, while Chinese, who are sober,
> or duly law abiding, clean, educated and in-
> dustrious, are shut out. There are few China-
> men in jails and none in the poor houses. There
> are no Chinese tramps or drunkards. Many
> Chinese here have become sincere Christians,
> in spite of the persecution which they have to
> endure from their heathen countrymen. More
> than half the Chinese in this country would

become citizens if allowed to do so, and would be patriotic Americans.[9]

But the law forbidding Chinese to become U.S. citizens was on the books; the Chinese Exclusion Act was followed by further restrictive measures. The Scott Act of 1888 prohibited Chinese workers from returning to America after a visit to China unless they had relatives in this country, or owned land worth $1,000—requirements that few could meet. The Exclusion Act was renewed in 1892 and again in 1902, this time for an indefinite period. In 1921 the United States denied all foreign-born women the right to share their husbands' citizenship. Then in 1924 the Johnson-Reed Act, or National Origins Act, placed strict limitations on the immigration of certain national groups, and totally prohibited the immigration of any persons "ineligible for citizenship." The Chinese, of course, fell within that classification.

The effects of these measures were devastating. Chinese men were devoted to their families. Their main purpose in coming to America was to fulfill their obligation to support their dependent relatives. Their sense of honor prevented them from returning home for good until they had earned enough to provide the comforts they had promised. Some, of course, had eventually earned the right to go home. But many struggled on, never quite managing to save enough. They would go home, briefly, once every four or five years, to see their families, and then return to the United States.

The Scott Act virtually put an end to this practice of occasional visits, while the Johnson-Reed Act prevented wives from coming to America to join their husbands. In effect, a whole generation of Chinese men was condemned to loneliness. Unmarried men fared just as badly as married men. They could not go to China, find a wife, and bring her to America because of the ban on immigration. At the same time, there were very few unmarried Chinese women in America, and intermarriage between Chinese men and white women was rare. Many states had laws prohibiting mixed marriages, and the Chinese themselves frowned on mixed marriages—based on the belief that the Chinese were superior to other races.

The cruelty of the new measures stunned the Chinese immigrants. A spokesman among them protested:

> I don't understand how the Government of the United States gave us such a law. Talk about friendship between the two countries! When an American goes to China, the Chinese people welcome him. Why we are getting this bad treatment I can't see. Can a man live in this country without a wife, never see his wife? I can't understand your new law breaking up the people in a family. . . . I can't make it out.[10]

Most Chinese immigrants had no choice but to stay on in America. They could not afford to go home. They just hoped that one day they would save enough to allow them to see their families again.

Many never did. But for some the Johnson-Reed Act of 1924 was the last straw. They had put up with hostility from the whites for a long time. Now, deprived of the right to be joined by their families, they decided that they'd had enough. Taking what money they had, they returned to China. Incredibly, some Americans condemned them for this.

Under the terms of the Exclusion Act, Chinese students, classified as temporary visitors, were still allowed to come to the United States for limited periods. But this caused problems. Once in America, some students, alarmed by the hostility of their white classmates, stopped going to college and disappeared into a Chinatown instead. As a result, the immigration officers in San Francisco were apt to be less than welcoming. Fu Chi Hao, a student who arrived in 1901, was told that his passport was not in order, and was placed in a detention shed. This he described in a magazine article:

> The detention shed is another name for a "Chinese jail." The interior is about one hundred feet square. Oftentimes they put in as many as two hundred human beings. . . . No friends are allowed to come in and see the unfortunate sufferers without special permission from the American authority. No letters are allowed either to be sent out or to come in. There are no tables, no chairs. We were treated like a group of animals, and we were fed on the floor. Kicking and swearing by the white man in charge was not a rare thing. I was not sur-

prised when, one morning, a friend pointed out to me the place where a heartbroken Chinaman had hanged himself after four months' imprisonment in this dreadful dungeon, this to end his agony and the shameful outrage.[11]

Because they had been deprived of the right to citizenship, the Chinese immigrants were denied the power of political protest against injustice. Only a limited number of jobs were open to them—cook, houseboy, and laundryman being the most common. They were barred from most other fields of employment, just as they were prevented from buying homes in white neighborhoods. Many lived their entire lives in their Chinese community—perpetual bachelors, cut off from their families and from the outside world.

There were some men who had wives and children. Born on American soil, the children were American citizens. Yet they, too, grew up in an atmosphere of discrimination and prejudice that was to persist for a long time.

# Chapter 5

# A Continuing Struggle

The racist campaign of harassment and discrimination against the Chinese went on for several decades, though in a less violent form. Peter Wong, a Chinese orphan who came to America in 1921 to join his uncle, learned about prejudice at an early age:

> As a child, I always felt I was Chinese, not an American. . . . My uncle would tell me whenever I went out, "Don't go too far because the white people are against you. They may throw a rock or do something to hurt you." I couldn't even get a haircut.[1]

California, the state with the largest Chinese population, was the most discriminatory. Peter Wong recalled that

> In California no Chinese could walk along with a white woman. No Chinese were allowed to go into a hospital even if they were sick.

45

People weren't allowed to hire Chinese or give
them a job in a factory. No Chinese could buy
land. No Chinese could buy a house, not in
California.[2]

Shunned by whites, many Chinese relied for their
livelihood on their fellow countrymen and on other
nonwhites. As Peter Wong explained:

I was working in my uncle's grocery store and
most of his trade was from the colored people,
not from the white people. White people didn't
trade with Chinese. . . . If it wasn't for the
colored people, the Chinese people couldn't
have stayed there because they're just like anybody else, they have to do something to make a
living. . . .

In all my life I always worked for the
Chinese, never for the Americans. I worked in
a laundry, I worked in a restaurant, I worked
in a Chinese grocery store, things like that.[3]

The Second World War marked a turning point
in the lives of the Chinese in America. China and
Japan had been at war since 1931, and at the out-
break of World War II, Japanese troops occupied
Peking, Shanghai, and other major Chinese cities.
The United States entered the war in 1941, after
Japan attacked Pearl Harbor. China and America
were, therefore, allies in the fight against Japan.

Almost immediately the Chinese exclusion laws
came under fire. Fair-minded people considered it
scandalous that Chinese men, who were fighting

alongside Americans, were not allowed to enter the United States. Besides, would it not boost China's morale if the United States were to make a friendly gesture to her ally? In 1943, after a long debate in Congress, President Franklin Delano Roosevelt finally signed an act repealing the Chinese exclusion laws. A strict limit was placed on the number of Chinese who could enter the United States—only 105 a year—but it was a start. At the same time, a few American employers, who believed it was wrong to discriminate against allies of the United States, began to accept Chinese for jobs that had been closed to them. And Uncle Sam allowed Chinese in the armed forces.

After the war China went through a civil war between the Nationalists, led by Chiang Kai-shek, and the Communists, under the leadership of Mao Tse-tung. Both groups raced to seize control of areas liberated by the withdrawal of Japanese troops. Defeated, the Nationalist leaders fled to the island of Taiwan, in December 1949, while the Communists established their capital at Peking and formed the People's Republic of China. The United States, fiercely anti-Communist, refused to recognize the Communist regime as the legal government of China, and kept it from representing China at the United Nations when it was formed.

Meanwhile, many Chinese refugees, fleeing from the Communists, flooded into Hong Kong. Those who wanted to come to America came up against quota restrictions. The United States did allow some five thousand Chinese women to enter the country under the War Brides Act of 1945, but a further seventeen years would pass before the majority of the refugees would gain admission. That it took so long was due, in large measure, to the isolationist and anti-Communist climate of the 1950s. Many Americans, mindful of Communist-inspired revolutions in other countries, wanted to avoid the possibility of similar conflicts in America. This, and the fear that too many foreigners would pour into America if the doors were opened, led to the passage of the McCarran-Walter Act in 1952. The act tightened up immigration controls and made the quota system more rigid.

By the early 1960s, however, the act was coming under fire from people who condemned the racist nature of the immigration laws. Ever since 1924, preference had been given to immigrants from northern Europe. This policy, originally based on the concept of Anglo-Saxon superiority, was now totally unacceptable to many Americans. They urged the government to adopt a more humanitarian and less racist policy toward immigration.

As a result, Congress passed a number of acts which overrode the quota restrictions. This enabled refugees from the 1956 Hungarian uprising, victims of earthquakes in the Azores, Cubans fleeing the Castro regime, and other "refugees, escapees, and expellees" to come to America. Also among the beneficiaries of new legislation were some fifteen thousand Chinese refugees whom President John F. Kennedy authorized to come to America from Hong Kong in 1962.

Three years later, in 1965, Congress passed new legislation which phased out the 1924 quota system altogether and replaced it with a new nonracist law. Under this new law, 170,000 immigrants a year could enter the United States from the Eastern Hemisphere, with no more than 20,000 from any one country. The Chinese took advantage of the change; between 1965 and 1970 over 75,000 entered the United States, and New York replaced San Francisco as the city to which most wanted to go.

For the Chinese who have come here since World War II, life has often been hard. Anti-Chinese prejudice, though not so violent or so widespread as during the late nineteenth century, still exists in some areas. The experience of Mary Ching, for example, who arrived in 1950 at the age of twenty-eight, was not unusual:

> The immigration officers were not very nice to us. They treated us like backwards people but I thought maybe they didn't understand our Chinese history, our traditions, our philosophy.
>
> I didn't expect prejudice. Prejudice is very hard for me to take. When you go into the store and you want to buy something they ignore you. When you ask questions about a different cut of meat, or something else, they make you feel like an idiot. "How come you don't know nothing? That's why you're Chinese people, you don't know nothing." This is very

insulting because each country is different and customs are different.[4]

Unlike the earlier Chinese immigrants, who always dreamed of returning home, most of the new immigrants intend to stay in America. They have, therefore, made a much greater effort than their predecessors to adapt to the American way of life. But at the same time, as Mrs. Ching explains, they hope to maintain some of their traditions:

> Our background is very different, and so we do think a little differently. When we are little our parents teach us to be humble, and then we teach our children to do their best, to give all that they have. I'm not going to change to please these prejudiced people. I shall do what I think is right and live by my principles.
>
> We still keep some of our traditional ways. As far as the children are concerned, for instance, we tell them, "We are the boss." Whatever they do, they have to consult us first, and then we make the decision for them.[5]

Most Chinese immigrants hope to preserve their traditionally close family ties when they come here. They find American attitudes hard to understand, as Ken Lee, who arrived in 1962, explained:

> Americans are always thinking of themselves: me, me, me—that's the only thing they know. If you have a longer culture, like us, then you think differently, you share your feelings, you share everything instead of being selfish. Back

in China, if you raise children, you expect them to support you later on. But here they don't even come back to see you. That's what American parents expect of their children.[6]

Many Chinese immigrants also hoped that their children would learn something of Chinese culture. To this end, special Chinese language schools were established. But, as one student pointed out, not all Chinese-Americans were enthusiastic.

The teacher devoted one hour each evening to our beginner's class, during which we were expected to grasp firmly the fundamentals of the language as well as rudimentary ideas of Chinese history, geography, and philosophy. For the remaining two hours we were left alone. We spent them memorizing our lessons aloud, drawing Chinese characters with smelly black ink and pencil-like bamboo paintbrushes, or, more frequently, reading Western novels and magazines . . . behind our Chinese textbooks.[7]

The attitude of the students illustrates a major difficulty in Chinese communities today. The older Chinese, who may be the China-born sons or grandsons of earlier immigrants, often cling to Chinese ways. They speak Chinese, wear Chinese clothes, eat Chinese food and live in Chinatowns or Chinese neighborhoods. Younger second- or third-generation Chinese-Americans, on the other hand, born in America and anxious to be like other Americans, have often broken away from their parents' traditional beliefs and have rebelled against studying their ancestral languages and customs. As a result, the traditional, tightly knit Chinese family, in which the father's word was law, is found less and less frequently.

In many cases communication between Chinese grandparents and their American-born grandchildren has become virtually impossible, since the former speak only Chinese and the latter only English. This is a dilemma that immigrants from most countries have faced, but for the Chinese, so proud of their ancient traditions, it is particularly hard to bear. Chinese-American author Calvin Lee illustrated the problem in his book about Chinatown:

> After a short visit by his grandmother, my four-year-old son announced at dinner that he was going to say "park the car" in Chinese. My wife, delighted with this first attempt into bilingualism, listened attentively as my son said, "Parkee car." Poor grandmother, she dies a thousand deaths as she sees in two short generations the complete loss of thousands of years of Chinese tradition. These children don't even know that they are Chinese.[8]

But even though the children think American, talk American, eat American, and dress American, they still look Chinese. And because of that, they tend to be singled out as "different" by their classmates. Ron Low, for instance, went through utter misery at his first school:

Elementary school was awful, I mean it really blew my mind. . . . Because we lived in a predominantly black area the school which I attended was also predominantly black. I was the only Asian attending the school at that time. My experience at this elementary school was pure hell. All the other kids referred to me as being white or non-black. The classic phrase of "Ching Chong Chinaman sitting on a fence, trying to make a dollar out of fifteen cents" was tossed at me constantly.[9]

Eventually Low's parents moved to a new area and he looked forward to going to an integrated school, where, he was sure, life would be a lot easier. It wasn't:

I still suffered the same rejections and hurts, but this time it was twice as bad. Not only did the blacks not accept me and considered me white, the whites wouldn't accept me either and labeled me non-white or even black on various occasions. I was in the middle as many other Asians were.[10]

Racist attitudes are by no means confined to the schoolroom. Despite the introduction of various laws to protect the rights of minority groups, some employers still refuse to take on Chinese workers, as Pardee Lowe, another first-generation Chinese-American, discovered when he went looking for a job:

Everywhere I was greeted with perturbation, amusement, pity or irritation—and always with identically the same answer. "Sorry," they invariably said, "the position has just been filled." My jaunty self-confidence soon wilted. I sensed something was radically, fundamentally wrong. It just didn't seem possible that overnight all of the positions could have been occupied, particularly not when everybody spoke of a labor shortage. Suspicion began to dawn. What had father said? "American firms do not customarily employ Chinese."[11]

That discrimination against the Chinese has continued for so long is due, to a large extent, to the creation of the Chinese stereotype by American writers and moviemakers. Whole generations of Americans, treated to utterly misleading portrayals of the Chinese, have formed opinions that have no basis in fact. Calvin Lee explains:

The image of the Chinese in America is a combination of stereotypes created by the early newspapers and magazines, and later added to by Hollywood. From 1920 to 1930 there was the image of Fu Manchu, evil and inscrutable. Later, when there was an era of good feeling toward the Chinese, the image was that of Charlie Chan, clever and patient. The advent of Communist China may have the effect of changing the image again to the evil and the inscrutable. Such a notion is utterly strange to the second, third, and fourth generation

Chinese-Americans. We are entering the professions and we feel as American as ham and eggs.[12]

Chinese-Americans who have entered the professions have often had to fight discrimination every step of the way. But today, thanks to a more enlightened attitude among some young Americans, Chinese-Americans are finding it easier to progress. Robert Eng Dunn, for instance, says that being Chinese has actually helped him to advance:

If Americans have called me names, so have the Chinese who speak of me scornfully as being a "native" and as knowing nothing of things Chinese. True, many Chinese regard me highly because I am a junior at Harvard; but I can say without ostentation that my American friends also respect me as a student. In fact, they give me more respect because I am Chinese. Whatever I do in school and college in the way of extracurricular activities or of attaining high grades, I am given much more credit and popularity than an American would receive if he did the same things. Being a Chinese among American friends is, then, a sort of advantage.[13]

But, as Robert Eng Dunn goes on to explain, there are also disadvantages. His assimilation into American society has led to a certain rejection on the part of his Chinese friends:

I feel the clash of cultures within me even now,
because I live with my father and I contact my
Chinese friends who represent the pure Chinese culture. My relatives are also of a different
background than myself, and they all advise
that I make friends, not for friendship's sake,
but with the hope that they will help me get a
job sometime. They object openly or become
suspicious when I am seen walking with a girl.
They pour contempt upon religion, especially
upon Christianity, and fail to see the precious-
ness and value of the individual life. This culture and attitude is contrary to mine, and I feel
I shall be unhappy in the process of yielding
to it.[14]

Most Chinese-Americans have faced a similar
dilemma. Torn between the demands of two different cultures, they have had to choose one at the
expense of the other. As a result, many Chinese-
Americans now face rejection, not from white Americans, but from the Chinese themselves. Laurence
Yep, in his novel *Child of the Owl,* illustrated this
problem. His heroine Casey, a Chinese-American
girl who, having been brought up as an American,
is unfamiliar with the Chinese language and with
Chinese ways, goes to live in San Francisco's Chinatown. On her first day at school her classmates poke
fun at her because she doesn't speak Chinese. Morti-
fied, she runs to the bathroom:

I saw myself in the mirror. My skin color and
different-shaped eyes were like theirs. Only I

didn't want to be like them because they made me feel rotten and fat and ugly. No one had ever made me feel like this when I was in the American schools outside of Chinatown. I felt like someone had made a mask out of the features of their faces and glued it over my real one so everyone would think I was as stupid and mean as those girls outside . . . those *Chinese* girls.[15]

In many respects, San Francisco's Chinatown has changed little over the years. It still has the colorful facades, the souvenir stores and restaurants, the traditional parades and celebrations. And it still has many of the problems that existed in the late nineteenth century. As Casey described it:

A lot of people lived in Chinatown because . . . they wanted to. But there were a lot of people who would have liked to live away from Chinatown if they could only speak enough English. Since they couldn't, they were stuck here, paying high rents for tiny apartments, even though they might have been able to get apartments of the same size some blocks away—that's assuming that the landlords would be fair-minded and rent to Chinese, and more landlords were being fair-minded nowadays. And those same Chinese couldn't get good-paying jobs for the same reason they couldn't move out of Chinatown so they wound up washing dishes and doing all the other dirty jobs in Chinatown and getting underpaid because they didn't even know what they ought to be earning.[16]

Poverty, unemployment, substandard housing, poor health, drug addiction, juvenile delinquency— these are all major problems in the Chinatowns of today.

A special strike force from the Department of Labor uncovered evidence in 1979 of violations of the Fair Labor Standards Act in thirty-five percent of the 500 New York Chinatown garment factories that were investigated. Violations included failure to keep records, failure to pay time-and-a-half wages for overtime, failure to pay the minimum wage of $2.90 an hour, and the employment of children. And as long as there are Chinese who insist on clinging to their language and customs, and who cannot, or will not, adapt to the American culture, these problems are likely to remain.

But to the majority of Chinese and Chinese-Americans, Chinatown belongs to the past. Thousands of people who grew up in Chinatown have now moved away. Today there are Chinese living in cities and towns across the nation. Many have been successful in business and the professions. There are Chinese politicians, scientists, Nobel prize winners, engineers, artists, and others who have achieved what their predecessors would have thought impossible.

In education, social life, and career opportunities, Chinese-Americans are experiencing fewer and fewer barriers. But discrimination still exists—that subtle form of discrimination that prevents Chinese from moving into certain neighborhoods, or from getting promotions that they deserve. In time these last barriers will be dismantled. But until then Chinese-Americans who, because of the color of their skin and the shape of their eyes, are still labeled by many as "foreigners" will have to continue to struggle for all their rights as Americans.

# FROM JAPAN

# Chapter 6

# Filling the Gap

On July 8, 1853, Commodore Matthew C. Perry of the United States Navy sailed into Tokyo Bay. He brought a message for the emperor of Japan from the President of the United States, proposing trade and friendship between America and Japan. Perry promised to return for an answer the following year.

For more than two hundred years Japan, like China, had been closed to the outside world. Its period of isolation began in the early seventeenth century when the powerful Tokugawa clan seized control and reduced the emperor's role to that of a figurehead. The Tokugawas, who ruled as shoguns, or military regents, wanted to put an end to the spread of Christianity in Japan, and of Western influence generally, which they saw as a threat to their authority. One of their first acts was, therefore, to expel all foreigners from Japan—mainly British, Spanish, and Portuguese traders and missionaries. They then closed all Japanese ports to foreign vessels

63

and forbade Japanese subjects to leave their country. To Westerners, Japan became an inaccessible, mysterious nation.

It was with the aim of bringing Japan out of her seclusion—and of providing American traders with a new market for their goods—that Commodore Perry set sail for Tokyo in 1853. Fortunately for Perry, he arrived at a time when Japan was in chaos. After two centuries of calm, the shogunate was under pressure from imperial supporters who were trying to regain power for the emperor. Unable to keep Perry out and fight the imperialists, the shogun allowed him to return. The American proposal was accepted, and a treaty opening up trade and other exchanges was signed.

Perry had brought with him a number of gifts for the emperor. They included tiny, model steam locomotives, modern guns and machinery, as well as one hundred gallons of the best Kentucky bourbon. The machinery and weapons had a devastating effect on Japanese society. Government officials were impressed by the sophisticated equipment. They realized that, if Japan were to compete as a trading nation, she would need to produce similar goods. They therefore launched a major program of industrialization. Giant factories and industrial complexes were built, and within fifty years Japan was transformed from a rural society into a highly industrialized and aggressive world power.

During the early stages of the Japanese transformation, the ban on emigration remained in force. The emperor, who was finally restored to power in

1868, knew about the treatment of the Chinese in California, and had no desire to see Japanese subjects treated the same way.

There were some exceptions, however. During the 1860s and 1870s a small number of Japanese students came to the United States to study. Among them were five young girls, aged between eight and fifteen, who were sent by the emperor as wards of Japan. The emperor's idea was that these girls, when they returned to Japan and married, would pass on to future generations what they had learned, and at the same time would improve the status of women in Japan. "As a little leaven leavens the whole lump, so would the education of women elevate the women of Japan." Such was the opinion of one Mr. Kuroda, whose enthusiasm had brought about the experiment.

An American education, and the success that would surely follow, became the dream of many a young Japanese boy, such as this one:

> The desire to see America was burning at my boyish heart. The land of freedom and civilization of which I heard so much from missionaries and the wonderful story of America I heard of those of my race who returned from here made my longing ungovernable. Meantime I have been reading a popular novel among the boys, "The Adventurous Life of Tsurukichi Tanaka, Japanese Robinson Crusoe." How he acquired new knowledge from America and how he is honored and favored by the capitalists in Japan. How willingly he has endured the

hardships in order to achieve the success. The story made a strong impression on my mind. Finally I made up my mind to come to this country to receive an American education.[1]

Finding the money for such an undertaking was not always easy, as the boy discovered. Although some of the Japanese students in America had wealthy parents, or government scholarships, others had to find some way of supporting themselves while they studied. Employment opportunities were not plentiful.

Great disappointment and regret I have experienced when I was told that I, the boy of 17 years old, smaller in stature indeed than an ordinary 14 years old American boy, imperfect in English knowledge, I can be any use here, but become a domestic servant, as the field for Japanese very narrow and limited. Thus reluctantly I have submitted to be a recruit of the army of domestic servants of which I never dreamed up to this time.[2]

American families who could not afford to employ full-time servants often employed Japanese students. They would offer them room and board and a couple of dollars a week, in exchange for a few hours' work a day. Well-to-do homes with a full-time staff of servants—usually Chinese and Irish—also hired Japanese students when they needed extra help. Most students had a hard time. They were not familiar with American ways, could not speak English, and were often given the dirtiest, heaviest jobs. The boy recalled the misery of his first day at work:

> When I first entered the kitchen wearing a white apron what an uncomfortable and mortifying feeling I experienced. I thought I shall never be able to proceed the work. I felt as if I am pressed down on my shoulder with loaded tons of weight. My heart palpitates. I did not know what I am and what to say. I stood by the door of kitchen motionless like a stone, with a dumbfounded silence. The cook gave me a scornful look and said nothing. Perhaps at her first glance she perceived me entirely unfit to be her help.[3]

In theory, part-time domestic work left the students with plenty of time to do their school work. In practice, it was a different matter:

> Some say Japanese are studying while they are working in the kitchen, but it is all nonsense. Many of them started so, but nearly all of them failed. . . . After you have served dinner, washing dishes and cleaning dining-room, you are often tired when you commence to write an essay. You will feel sometime your fingers are stiff and your arms ache. In the afternoon, just when you began concentrated on the points in the book, the front door bell rung—the goods delivered from the stores, or callers to mistress. . . . I have experience, once I attended lecture after I have done a rush work in the

kitchen. I was so tired felt as though all the
blood in the body rushing up to the brain and
partly sleepy. My hands would not work. I
could not take the note of professor's lecture,
as my head so dull could not order to my hand
what professor's lecture was.[4]

While these students toiled in the kitchens of America, the Japanese government gave permission for
some two thousand citizens to go to Hawaii—at that
time an independent kingdom—during the early
1880s. The sugar and pineapple planters there were
expanding their operations and were badly in need
of extra workers. The Hawaiian government had
sent a message to Japan stating that

> this Government is prepared to provide free
> passage for Japanese agricultural workers or
> domestic servants, with their wives . . . and a
> certain number of their children. . . . The emi-
> grants shall not be required to contract for
> service beforehand, neither shall they be under
> any obligation to enter into service on arrival
> here, but the Government will on their part
> undertake to find them employment on one or
> other of our plantations at rates not less than a
> reasonable minimum to be fixed before the emi-
> grant leaves Japan.[5]

The need for agricultural workers was all the greater
after the passage of the Chinese Exclusion Act of
1882. The act was passed at a time when the plantations of both Hawaii and California were expanding

rapidly. The growers needed a steady supply of new labor and when the Chinese were banned from immigrating, they had to look for another group to take their place.

At the time Japan was suffering from acute overcrowding. In 1886 the emperor finally lifted the ban on emigration, even going so far as to encourage it from the most densely populated areas.

There was no shortage of Japanese who were willing to pack their bags and go. Japan's transition from agriculture to industry was then under way. The farming community, which had lived off the land for generations, resented the change. Many could see no hope of succeeding in a country that was being swallowed up by giant industrial complexes. In Hawaii and California, though, it seemed that they might be able to make the fortunes that eluded them at home. A steady stream of Japanese began to cross the Pacific.

Immigration companies in Hawaii and California were soon set up to make the necessary arrangements. Some of the earlier immigrants acted as brokers, set up boardinghouses and hotels to welcome the newcomers, met them at the docks and allocated jobs. This notice appeared in the *Hawaiian-Japanese Chronicle*:

> Great recruiting to America. Through an arrangement made with Yasumaza, of San Francisco, we are able to recruit laborers to the mainland and offer them work. The laborers will be subjected to no delay upon arriving in

San Francisco, but can get work immediately
through Yasumaza. Employment offered in
picking strawberries and tomatoes, planting
beets, mining and domestic service. Now is the
time to go! Wages $1.50 a day.[6]

At that time the average laborer's wage in Japan was
about fourteen cents a day, so the promise of $1.50
a day was very attractive, even though, by American standards, it was a low wage.

The Japanese arrived in time to fill the gap
created by the Chinese Exclusion Act. In addition
to providing the much-needed farm labor, the Japanese worked in mines, on the railroads, and in private homes as domestics and gardeners. Others
established businesses to cater to their countrymen.

Before long, an area of Los Angeles became
known as Little Tokyo. For the Japanese, like other
immigrant groups, established their own community
—a place where they could relax with their com-
patriots. An immigrant who lived in Little Tokyo
explained some of its attractions:

Japanese farmers and laborers came to Little
Tokyo for lots of reasons . . . especially to get
things from Japan. They would even use many
of the large dry goods and grocery firms as
banks because they did not understand the
language at American banks. . . . Nowadays,
even big chain stores carry Japanese foods but
in the old days you can't even get rice outside
of Little Tokyo . . . but not only food, but
things like clothes. Japanese were small and

skinny, and it was hard to find suits for them outside of Little Tokyo.[7]

As with Chinatown, the immigrant went on, there was also a darker side to Little Tokyo:

> Much to the discomfort of the more conservative individuals within the community, the drinking bars and the large vice quarters (Los Angeles had an extensive and infamous red light district during the 1900 period) proved to be a powerful attraction to many of [the] young men, especially after a hard day's work on farm fields and orchards or with the railroad. Gambling, too, proved to be a major source of diversion . . . and indications are that it played a large role in the "development" of Little Tokyo.[8]

Most of the issei, as the first Japanese immigrants were called, were young unmarried men. And many, like the Chinese, planned to make their fortunes and return home. But there were also some who had managed to find enough money to bring their wives and families with them, and who planned to settle in the United States. This made the first Japanese seem more respectable to the Californians than the Chinese; they were intelligent, hardworking, and had some education.

By the turn of the century there were over twenty-five thousand Japanese in the United States. Many had been successful and had established thriving businesses.

But they had also made enemies in California.

# Chapter 7

# "The Japs Must Go!"

It didn't take long for the color-conscious Californians to react to the influx of Japanese immigrants. As early as 1892 Dennis Kearney was back on the steps of San Francisco's City Hall with a revised refrain. This time "The Japs Must Go!" At a mass meeting in 1900, calling for the extension of the Chinese Exclusion Act to include the Japanese as well, the mayor of San Francisco stated that

> the Japanese are starting the same tide of immigration which we thought we had checked twenty years ago. . . . The Chinese and Japanese are not bona fide citizens. They are not the stuff of which American citizens are made. . . . Personally we have nothing against Japanese but as they will not assimilate with us and their social life is so different from ours, let them keep at a respectful distance.[1]

The old racist argument—that the Japanese could never be assimilated into the great American melting pot—found widespread support. But the attacks on the Japanese were also based on economic fears. More ambitious than the Chinese, the Japanese soon made it clear that they were not prepared to work as laborers forever. They had come to America to make a fortune and they would do everything in their power to achieve it. Their families and communities expected it of them. The status of the family name depended on it. As Noriko Oma, a modern-day immigrant, explains, Japanese society did not tolerate failure:

> The first immigrants who came to this country came for economic gain. They came with that dream and worked very hard for success. Because this is the Japanese culture. You go out and either you are going to die, or come back with success. You don't come back as a failure. When you go to war, you either come back dead, or in victory.[2]

The Japanese also had a great knowledge of farming. Japan is made up of over three thousand islands. Much of the land is mountainous; less than one fifth of it is level enough for cultivation. As a result, the Japanese had learned, over the centuries, to make the best possible use of what little land they had. When they came to California, they saw land being wasted. Knowing that they could make a fortune out of that land, they set about making enough money to become independent farmers.

By consistently underbidding white workers for labor contracts, the Japanese were able to monopolize the farm labor market. Then, once they had eliminated most of the competition, the Japanese demanded higher wages. They were able to save and, eventually, buy or lease their own land.

Reclaiming vast areas of swampland, which had been considered useless by the Californians, the Japanese concentrated on high-profit crops that relied on manpower rather than machinery. Before long they were producing most of California's strawberries, peppers, celery, tomatoes, grapes, and many other commodities. They also showed Americans how to grow rice. California farmers had failed in their efforts to produce rice, but the Japanese, with their greater understanding of the plant and of soil properties, established successful rice plantations. Some years later, in 1919, the Japanese Association of America expressed pride in this achievement:

The Japanese were not the first to try rice in California, but they were the first to make it a commercial proposition. . . . And they were the ones to stick to rice through all the years before the industry emerged from its uncertainties and became firmly established. The Japanese demonstrated success and the American farmers, who have since been getting rich out of the industry . . . must admit their prosperity is founded on a structure thrown up by the daring and persistence of the Japanese.[3]

But the Japanese received little praise from Californians for their achievements. California farmers considered it a personal affront that the "little brown men," whom they believed to be racially inferior, should have demonstrated a superiority as farmers. They were also horrified at the amount of land that was falling into Japanese hands. California, they claimed, would soon be overrun by the Japanese unless something was done to keep them out.

In fact, the number of Japanese coming to America was relatively small. It reached a peak during the first decade of the twentieth century, when over 125,000 came, but that was very few compared with the millions of foreigners who were pouring in from Italy, Hungary, Russia, and other European countries at the same time. But, like the Chinese, the Japanese looked "different," and most of them lived on the West Coast.

In 1906 the San Francisco Board of Education tried to confine all Asians to segregated schools—which attracted national and international attention. Japanese immigrants, always more prepared to fight discrimination than the more docile Chinese, protested vehemently. How, they asked, could their children ever learn American ways if they were not allowed to mix with other Americans? Why, when the main argument against the Japanese was that they could not be assimilated, were Americans closing one of the main avenues toward assimilation?

The segregation proposal affected Chinese as well as Japanese children, but the events that followed were concerned mainly with Japan. The Japanese government had always shown more concern for the welfare of its citizens abroad than the Chinese. China had been too preoccupied with wars and internal rebellion to pay much attention to what was happening in America.

As soon as it heard about the board of education proposal, the Japanese government lodged an official protest in Washington. By this time Japan was a major world power; the protest could not be ignored. But how was President Theodore Roosevelt to placate the Japanese without antagonizing the Californians, whose support he needed?

Recognizing that the school issue was only a small part of the problem, he negotiated the famous "Gentlemen's Agreement" with Japan. Signed in 1908, the agreement was essentially a compromise, saving face on both sides. California was forced to back down on the segregation issue, and Japan agreed to limit emigration to those who already had relatives in the United States.

These measures did little, however, to reduce anti-Japanese feeling on the West Coast. The Japanese were victimized by discriminatory laws in several states, and then, in 1913, California passed the Alien Land Act. This stated that aliens ineligible for citizenship could not own land. The Japanese, like the Chinese, had always been barred from citizenship. To the dismay of the anti-Japanese agitators, however, the law did not have the desired effect. The ingenious issei got around it by buying land in the name of their American-born children, called nisei, who were citizens of the United States. By 1919 over seventy-four thousand Japanese owned land.

Why, in the face of so much hostility, did the Japanese stay? Why didn't they go back to Japan? The reason is that, like immigrants from the world over, the issei had come to consider America as their home:

> We live here. We have cast our lot with California. We are drifting farther and farther away from the traditions and ideas of our native country. Our sons and daughters do not know them at all. They do not care to know them. They regard America as their home.
>
> We have little that binds us to Japan. Our interest is here, and our fortune is irrevocably wedded to the state in which we have been privileged to toil and make a modest contribution to the development of its resources. What is more important, we have unconsciously adapted ourselves to the ideals and manners and customs of our adopted country, and we no longer entertain the slightest desire to return to our native country.[4]

These were the words of George Shima, "the Japanese Potato King." Shima, who came to America in 1890, had made a fortune out of growing potatoes after draining a vast area of swampland. He claimed that the Japanese, especially those with wives and children here, were committed to America. Most Chinese immigrants, on the other hand, clung on to the hope of returning to China. As a result, he said, they were much less willing than the Japanese to adapt to the American way of life.

In 1920, when Shima was president of the Japanese Association of America, he stated:

> It seems to me wrong and unjust to propose various measures, calculated to oppress and inflict hardship upon the local Japanese, for the purpose of checking Japanese immigration.
>
> I don't like the man who puts the cart before the horse. If the present immigration arrangement with Japan is not satisfactory, there is a right way to find a remedy, and the right way is not to abuse and oppress the local Japanese, who are neither responsible for nor in a position to control Japanese immigration.[5]

His plea for fairness was followed by a warning:

> The constant exploitation of the Japanese question makes it well-nigh impossible for self-respecting Japanese to live in California. The result, I fear, is that eventually only the undesirable class of Japanese, who care not a straw for self-respect or dignity, will remain here. Certainly this cannot be the condition which California wishes to establish.[6]

Such reasonableness went unheeded. Californians had another axe to grind. After the signing of the 1908 Gentlemen's Agreement, most new Japanese immigrants were women, and of these a large proportion consisted of "picture brides." It was Japanese practice for a single man living in America to have a marriage arranged by relatives living in Japan. He would send a picture of himself to the woman in Japan whom he wanted to marry. She, in turn, sent a photograph to him, and if both parties agreed, their marriage was registered in Japan. The new bride then came to join her husband.

This was normal practice for the Japanese, who were accustomed to arranged marriages, but the Californians read something sinister into it. Japan was a major world power, a possible threat to the security of the United States. The picture brides, claimed the Californians, were a means of swelling the Japanese population in America—a kind of fifth column that would be ready to strike when the time came. As stated in the *Sacramento Bee*:

> The intent on the part of the Japanese, it is quite evident, now is to secure upon this continent a foothold for their race, not as individual units to be absorbed and assimilated in the great American melting pot, but as a compact body of loyal subjects of the Mikado [ancient title of emperor of Japan], to serve his interests in every way possible. For years the Japanese in California have been appealed to by their leaders and their vernacular newspapers "to beget many children and to secure much land" as the surest means for "permanently establishing [their] race in this country."[7]

Japan had fought on the Allied side during World War I, and Japanese men living in America had fought in the United States Armed Forces. But the complaints against picture brides continued until, in 1920, Japan agreed to stop issuing passports to the brides.

The only place where the Japanese did not find prejudice was Hawaii, which had become United States territory in 1900. Between 1886, when the first Japanese laborers arrived there, and 1908, when the Gentlemen's Agreement curtailed immigration, about 180,000 Japanese were brought to Hawaii as contract laborers. Some returned to Japan when their contracts expired, some moved to the United States mainland, but over a third chose to stay.

Compared with California, Hawaii was a haven for the Japanese. With its unique blend of races, languages, religions, and cultures (the Hawaiian population was made up of Polynesians, Chinese, Japanese, and Caucasians), there was no dominant majority. The government, concerned about the prosperity of its sugar and pineapple plantations, took good care of the Japanese laborers, appointing inspectors, interpreters, and doctors to look after them.

As a result, the Japanese in Hawaii had much better opportunities for advancement than those living elsewhere in the United States. There was no discrimination to prevent them from moving up the economic ladder, so by the 1920s many had become independent farmers and businessmen, or had entered the professions. In time the Japanese would become the wealthiest and most influential people in Hawaii.

But in California, of course, it was a different matter. By the early 1920s a good number of nisei had reached manhood. Well-educated and ambitious, they wanted very much to be part of America. They began to move away from their Japanese communities and into the mainstream of American life. This caused more trouble. The nisei, claimed the incensed Californians, were taking jobs away from whites in many businesses. The old "yellow peril" threat was brought out and aired again. West Coast politicians took note, and brought influence to bear on Washington.

The upshot was that in 1924 the Asian Exclusion Act was passed, aimed principally at the Japanese, since the Chinese were already excluded. This broke the Gentlemen's Agreement and decreed total exclusion for all aliens ineligible for citizenship. The Japanese government was shocked. It had always been willing to agree to American demands to restrict emigration, but to have its citizens barred from the United States was a blow to Japanese national prestige.

And some historians believe that the Exclusion Act, by the resentment it caused, prompted Japan to turn its back on the West and embark on military aggression in Asia. Eventually this would lead to war with the United States.

# Chapter 8

# The New Yellow Peril

Prejudice against the Japanese in America did not die out after the ban on further immigration. It festered for years until, in 1941, it erupted into unprecedented hatred and fury. For on December 7 of that year Japanese planes bombed Pearl Harbor in Hawaii.

For two years the United States had been hampering Japanese efforts to expand into Southeast Asia and to complete its conquest of China by cutting off supplies of oil and other essential raw materials. Japanese leaders finally decided that they would either have to give up hope of expanding their empire, or go to war with America. They chose the latter course and sent their warplanes to Pearl Harbor, where the U.S. Pacific fleet was based.

The attack came as a complete surprise to Americans. As the news flashed across the nation, everybody was stunned. It just didn't seem possible. Daniel Inouye, a Japanese-American living in Honolulu, who was later to become U.S. senator from Hawaii, recalls that awful day:

> I remember that I was buttoning my shirt and looking out of the window—it would be a magnificent day; already the sun had burned off the morning haze and glowed bright in a blue sky —when the hum of the warming [radio] set gave way to a frenzied voice. "This is no test!" the voice cried out. "Pearl Harbor is being bombed by the Japanese! I repeat: this is not a test or a maneuver! Japanese war planes are attacking Oahu!"
>
> . . . I could feel blood hammering against my temple, and behind it the unspoken protest, like a prayer—*It's not true! It* is *a test, or a mistake! It can't be true!*[1]

Within a few hours the Japanese had virtually wiped out the U.S. Pacific fleet, and with it any hopes that the issei and nisei may have had of being accepted in America. Reeling from the shock, Inouye jumped on his bicycle and raced off to a first-aid station to help the wounded!

> An old Japanese grabbed the handlebars of my bike as I tried to maneuver around a cluster of people in the street. "Who did it?" he yelled at me. "Was it the Germans? It must have been the Germans!"
>
> I shook my head, unable to speak, and tore free of him. My eyes blurred with tears, tears of pity for that old man, because he could not

accept the bitter truth, tears for all these frightened people. . . . They had worked so hard.
They had wanted so desperately to be accepted,
to be good Americans. And now, in a few
cataclysmic minutes, it was all undone, for in
the marrow of my bones I knew that there was
only deep trouble ahead.[2]

Until that moment Inouye had overlooked the fact
that he, too, was one of those people:

It came to me at last that I would face that
trouble too, for my eyes were shaped just like
those of that poor old man in the street, and
my people were only a generation removed
from the land that had spawned those bombers,
the land that sent them to rain destruction on
America, death on Americans. And choking
with emotion, I looked up into the sky and
called out, "You dirty Japs!"[3]

Anti-Japanese racists lost no time in raising once
more the cry of yellow peril. Pearl Harbor, they
claimed, proved that the Japanese-Americans were
a fifth column. Wild stories began to circulate.
Rumor had it that a huge Japanese fishing fleet was
operating off the coast of California, ready to be
converted into war vessels. The Japanese, claimed
another report, were cutting arrow-shaped markers
in the sugarcane fields of California to guide fighter
planes to their targets. No such allegations were ever
proved true, but they were enough to alarm.
  Within hours of the Pearl Harbor attack the FBI

had rounded up over five thousand Japanese-Americans—community leaders, organization heads, anybody in a position of authority. A witness to these indiscriminate pickups recalled that the FBI

> picked up anybody that was the head of anything. The same thing they did when Lenin and the Communists took over in Russia. . . . Just because we come from the same country, we get together occasionally, see, and just have a social time and talk about our friends back in Japan. But everyone that was the head of anything was picked up, which was a crazy thing.[4]

The FBI investigators released most of the suspects after ransacking their homes and interrogating them. The searches revealed no evidence that Japanese spies and saboteurs were at work in California. Nevertheless, the American public remained unconvinced. No "Jap" was to be trusted. The Chinese, who ran the risk of being mistaken for Japanese, took to wearing buttons stating "I Am Chinese."

During the weeks after Pearl Harbor, Japanese were dismissed from their jobs; their licenses to practice law and medicine were taken away; fishermen were barred from taking their boats out. California drivers sported windshield stickers saying "Remember a Jap Is a Jap." Other stickers urged Americans to "Slap a Jap Rat." Daily life became a nightmare for the Japanese. Grocers wouldn't sell them food; banks wouldn't honor their checks; gas stations refused them gas; hospitals refused to admit them. There were signs in barbershop windows read-

ing "Japs Shaved. Not Responsible for Accidents."
Restaurant windows sported "This Management Poi-
sons Both Rats and Japs."

The press, tolerant at first, soon became caught
up in the general hysteria. Syndicated columnist
Henry McLemore, for example, wrote in a column
that went out all over the country:

> I am for the immediate removal of every Japa-
> nese on the West Coast to a point deep in the
> interior. I don't mean a nice part of the in-
> terior either. Herd 'em up, pack 'em off, and
> give them the inside room in the badlands. Let
> 'em be pinched, hurt, hungry, and dead up
> against it. . . . Personally, I hate the Japanese.
> And that goes for all of them.[5]

The idea of imprisoning the Japanese found favor
in many quarters. Military leaders responsible for
the security of the West Coast were disturbed by the
presence of these "enemy aliens." After Pearl Harbor
the Japanese had landed in the Philippines and for
a while it was feared that they would invade the
United States mainland. By the end of December
this apprehension had largely subsided, but concern
about possible sabotage and espionage by Japanese-
Americans remained.

West Coast racists lost no time in calling for the
removal of the Japanese. They made no distinction
between the issei and the nisei. In their view, "A
Jap was a Jap," and all Japanese were treacherous
by nature.

Mixed with the racism and mistrust was an ele-

Of the ten thousand men who built the Central Pacific Railroad, nine thousand were Chinese. (Courtesy of the Collection of the Asian-American Research Institute of New York City.)

When news of the California gold strike reached China, men were ready to pull up stakes and go prospecting. (Courtesy of The New-York Historical Society, New York City.)

Wherever the Chinese went, they were mistreated and harassed. A newspaper cartoon shows the hanging of a Chinese in effigy. (Courtesy of the Collection of the Asian-American Research Institute of New York City.)

"Our Home Heathen—Teaching the 'Heathen Chinee.'" Learning the English language in a schoolroom. (Wood engraving. Frank Leslie's *Sunday Magazine*, 1881. Courtesy of the Collection of the Asian-American Research Institute of New York City.)

"Is it the religion of the Chinese residents in America of which you complain? What right have you to do this . . . ?" (Altar in the Chinese Joss-House, San Francisco. *Harper's Weekly,* 1871. Courtesy of The New York Public Library Picture Collection.)

There were some men who had wives and children. Affluent Chinese at home, c. 1900. (Courtesy of the Museum of the City of New York.)

Shunned by whites, many Chinese relied on their fellow countrymen. Chinese police, c. 1900. (Courtesy of the Museum of the City of New York.)

A group of Chinese boys in the Five Points House of Industry, New York. (Courtesy of the Collection of the Asian-American Research Institute of New York City.)

The tongs challenged the Six Companies for total control of Chinatown. Pell Street, c. 1910. (Courtesy of the Collection of the Asian-American Research Institute of New York City.)

The beginning of a new life. San Francisco Immigration Station, 1923. (Courtesy of the Collection of the Asian-American Research Institute of New York City.)

Hollywood helped create the stereotype of the Chinese in America. When there was an era of good feeling, the image was that of Charlie Chan, clever and patient. (Charlie Chan in *Dead Men Tell* [Sidney Toler and Sen Yung]. A Warner Bros.-Seven Arts photo.)

A Yank overseas, June
1942. (Courtesy of the
Collection of the Asian-
American Research Institute
of New York City.)

The first landing of Americans in Japan under Commodore Perry in 1853. (Lithograph. Courtesy of The New-York Historical Society, New York City.)

The Japanese provided much-needed farm labor at $1.50 a day. Japanese apple pickers, 1907. (Courtesy of Visual Communications, Asian-American Studies Central, Inc.)

A large proportion of Japanese women immigrants were "picture brides," seen here in San Francisco in 1919. (Courtesy of Visual Communications, Asian-American Studies Central, Inc.)

After Pearl Harbor, the Japanese on the West Coast were evacuated to internment camps in 1942. Rumor had it that they might be allowed to return to their homes when the war was ended. The proprietor of a barbershop in Seattle expressed his sentiments about that. (U.P.I.)

Some 117,000 Japanese-Americans were moved away from their homes and interned. Of these, 70,000 were nisei—citizens of the United States. Special camps were built in the desert. Manzanar in a dust storm. (National Archives.)

In many instances, families were given less than forty-eight hours to get ready. They had no idea what they would need, or how long they would be gone. (National Archives.)

Some Japanese were able to leave their homes or businesses in the care of friends, but most had to find buyers. (National Archives.)

Many thanks for your Patronage. Hope to Serve you in Near future God be with you till we meet again. Mr. and Mrs. K. Iseri

The barracks were partitioned into six rooms: one room for each family, provided with a stove, a light, and beds. Nothing else. (National Archives.)

Through all the humiliation and anguish, the majority of Japanese-Americans maintained a strong loyalty to the U.S. In 1943 the Army agreed to accept nisei volunteers. Twenty-six thousand Japanese-Americans served in the armed forces. (National Archives.)

Filipinos, believing the Americans would help in their struggle for independence, fought alongside the Americans in the Philippines in the Spanish-American War. Filipino Freedom Fighters, c. 1898. (Courtesy of the *Filipino Reporter*.)

Wherever they went, the Filipinos were victimized by ruthless employers. They would drift from farm to farm, harvesting crops. California grape pickers in 1936. (Courtesy of Visual Communications, Asian-American Studies Central, Inc.)

Most Filipinos tried to make the best of their time in America. They liked fine clothes, fast cars, and gambling. Two Filipinos in San Francisco, 1936. (Courtesy of Visual Communications, Asian-American Studies Central, Inc.)

When the Vietnam War came to an end in April 1975, thousands of refugees struggled to get out of Vietnam. Here an American official punches a man to get him out of the doorway of an overloaded evacuation plane. (U.P.I.)

Some Vietnamese resorted to boats. Every kind of vessel, ranging from small fishing boats to large cargo vessels, was used to ferry the refugees away from Vietnam. Some would be refused admission to overcrowded refugee camps elsewhere. (U.P.I.)

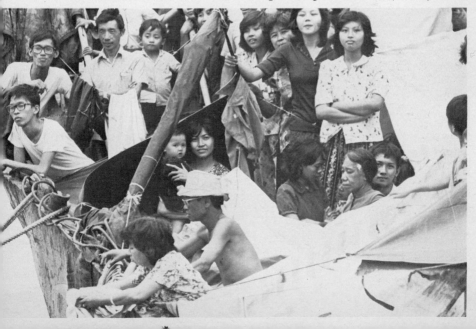

Life in the U.S. has meant low-paying jobs, language problems, and "culture shock" for many Vietnamese refugees. Nguyen Cao Ky, once the powerful premier of South Vietnam, ran a liquor-delicatessen-grocery store near Los Angeles in 1977. (U.P.I.)

ment of greed. Among the loudest supporters of internment were the California farmers. The removal of the Japanese would give them the chance to get their hands on the vast acreages of rich, Japanese-owned land.

Japanese-Americans tried to defend themselves. The nisei, in particular, were horrified to find themselves branded as the enemy. They were American citizens. Most had never been to Japan; most could not even speak Japanese. Time and again they swore that they were loyal to the United States. They gave money to buy bombers; they tried to enlist in the U.S. armed services but discovered that they were unacceptable. They tried getting help from their congressmen, only to discover that West Coast congressmen were calling for evacuation.

The issue was heatedly debated for several weeks. The government was reluctant to take the dramatic step of imprisoning Japanese-Americans. To do so would be unconstitutional and racist, for nobody had suggested rounding up Germans and Italians who were just as much "enemy aliens" as the Japanese. But finally, under the combined pressure of military advisors, West Coast politicians, and civilian groups, the government acted.

On February 9, 1942, President Franklin Delano Roosevelt signed Executive Order 9066. All persons of Japanese ancestry were to be moved away from the West Coast into special relocation camps. Altogether, some 117,000 Japanese-Americans were forced to leave their homes. Of these, 70,000 were nisei—citizens of the United States.

# Chapter 9

# Prisoners

Shortly after President Roosevelt signed the internment order, official notices were posted in the Japanese communities on the West Coast. Addressed to "all persons of Japanese ancestry," they ordered Japanese families to assemble at one of fifteen specified places at certain times, and to bring only those belongings that they could carry. In many instances families were given less than forty-eight hours to get ready. They had no idea what they would need, or how long they would be gone. Roy Yano, a young issei, recalled the misery of trying to prepare for the unknown:

> The government didn't tell us whether we would be able to come back or not. They didn't promise us anything. So I told my wife that perhaps the best thing would be to sell our furniture and buy food and medicines and things like that. Our younger daughter was only four

months old, and the older one was four years
old, and we didn't know if there would be doctors or hospitals in the camp. So we took in as
much medicine and baby food as possible.[1]

With so little time to dispose of their possessions,
homes, and businesses, the Japanese-Americans had
no choice but to accept low prices for their property.
Some were able to leave their homes or businesses in
the care of friends, but most had to find buyers. Bar-
gain hunters, thieves, and swindlers rushed in to get
what they could. Roy Yano described one bitter
encounter:

> There were a group of vultures who came
> in, knowing that we had to leave. . . . We had
> this brand new mangle. . . . We'd only bought
> it about a month before this. Now this man
> came in and saw it and offered me $5. We paid
> about $130 for it and he offered me $5. I told
> him what we paid and said we'd only used it a
> few times. He said he'd give us $10. By that
> time I got really mad and I said I'd rather give
> it to someone who would just say thank you.
> So he said, "Well I'll give you $50." I was so
> mad I said "Get out!"[2]

Everybody lost something in the evacuation; many
lost everything they had. One old man reflected
sadly:

> All we wanted to do was to be left alone on the
> coast. . . . My wife and I lost $10,000 in that
> evacuation. She had a beauty parlor and had

to give that up. I had a good position worked
up as a gardener, and was taken away from
that. We had a little home and that's gone
now.[3]

The first stops were for the evacuees temporary as-
sembly centers—racetracks, fairgrounds, stadiums,
and the like—while the army hastily built ten huge
relocation camps. By mid-June the first camps were
ready, and trains carried the prisoners to their new
homes—rows of desolate barracks surrounded by
barbed wire.

There were two camps in California, two in Arizona, two in Arkansas, one in Utah, one in Wy-
oming, one in Colorado, and one in Idaho. They
ranged in size from eight thousand inhabitants at
Granada, Colorado, to twenty thousand inhabitants
at Poston, Arizona. All the camps, except the two
in Arkansas, were built in the desert. As a result:
dust. According to Roy Yano:

These barracks were built in such a hurry that
there was no paved road or anything like that.
It was just full of dust. Every time you walked
all that powder would fly up and from top to
bottom we were covered with that white powder. . . . And inside our room too, no matter
how many times you dusted off, in half an hour
the inside was just full of dust again.[4]

The camps were divided into sections. Each section was made up of twelve barracks, a dining hall,
a recreation building, and a sanitation building

which housed toilets, showers, and laundry rooms. The Japanese, particularly the women, hated the sanitation buildings, which allowed them no privacy. Hila Shirasowa explained:

> We had the same bathroom, same showers, and nothing to divide us. You have all to stand and take a shower in one room. And the lavatory was the same way; there was no partition where you sat. But later, you know, people that do carpentry put partitions in between the seats.[5]

The barracks were partitioned into six rooms: one room for each family, provided with a stove, a light, and beds. Nothing else. It was up to each family to find some way to improve its surroundings, as Roy Yano explained:

> The barrack was built in such a way that there was no ceiling above each room—just one high ceiling. So what happened was that when someone at the end would light up, the whole barrack would light up. . . . When a person cannot have privacy, that is really bad. For myself, my children were young and it didn't matter too much, but I felt sorry for the people with teenage children. The first thing I can remember was when a lot of bread and vegetables were carted in in cardboard boxes and things like that. You ought to have seen those people go after those cardboard boxes! They used them to make partitions so as to make a little privacy.[6]

Gradually each camp became a community in which everyone worked to create a "normal" pattern of life. Roy Yano and Hila Shirasowa described some of the camp activities:

> The first thing we did in our camp—we built our churches. The Buddhist people got together and built their Buddhist church, and the Christian people built their own church. And the older Nisei who were out of college or high school, they started teaching the children. And so we set up schools. . . . Pretty soon the young people started playing baseball . . . and it was just like outside.[7]

> We all had jobs to do. They needed waiters and waitresses in the mess hall, and they needed dishwashers and cooks. And then we had adult education. They were trying to teach the Isseis English. There were recreation halls that taught the children basketball and baseball and swimming.[8]

> People started doing gardening and carpentry, and there were other things that people did too. They started something different because they were in a new situation. Some people felt they should raise vegetables, so they started turning the soil in between the barracks. For the doctors and dentists they had clinics. They examined the patients free of charge, naturally. And I think they received a minimum pay of $16 a month from the government.[9]

In spite of all the prisoners did to make life bearable, the strain was still too much. Daniel Okimoto, who was a child at the time, later recalled some of the bitter aspects of camp life:

> The . . . usual pattern of living was radically changed when the entire family was squeezed together in the same small room, separated only by a thin wall from the occupants of the neighboring unit. There everything a family said or did could be overheard and the most important question in life came to be: how much longer would one be trapped in the desert prison. Underlying tensions occasionally erupted into heated quarrels, emotional arguments, and petty bickering over trivia.[10]

The weeks dragged into months, and the months into years. Some Japanese were to spend almost three years in the camps—three tedious years in which, as Okimoto put it,

> everything was rigidly regimented and monotonous: the same buildings, always the familiar surroundings, set hours for meals, regular routines, prescribed procedures, the next day the same as the one before. Daily existence was devoid of the pleasure of surprise; the greatest excitement each day—for some the only thing to look forward to—was mail delivery.[11]

Through all the humiliation and anguish the majority of Japanese-Americans maintained a strong loyalty to the United States. Indeed, many nisei

begged for a chance to prove their loyalty by fighting in the armed forces. At first the Army refused to
take them on, considering it too risky to engage
people whose loyalty to the United States was doubt-
ful. But Japanese-American leaders persisted and
finally their efforts bore fruit. In 1943 the Army
agreed to accept nisei volunteers. Daniel Okimoto
reflected:

> The choice put before the twenty-year-old
> Japanese American was simple: either stay be-
> hind barbed wire for an indefinite period of
> time or go out into the battlefronts to fight for
> the country that had imprisoned him. . . .
>     When interned nisei asked whether risking
> their lives would facilitate the release of their
> families, the government's answer was an un-
> equivocal no. Nevertheless a large number of
> Japanese Americans volunteered for the army.[12]

Why, then, did the nisei volunteer? Quite simply,
they believed that only by fighting for America could
they convince the American public that they, too,
were Americans. In all, some twenty-six thousand
Japanese-Americans served in the armed forces,
many of them in the all-nisei 442nd Regimental
Combat Team. This unit fought with great heroism
and was one of the most decorated units in the entire military history of the United States.

At the end of the war, at a ceremony post-
humously awarding the Distinguished Service Cross
to Sergeant Kazuo Masuda, who had been killed

while fighting in Italy, General "Vinegar Joe" Stilwell said:

> The Nisei bought an awful big hunk of America with their blood. You're damn right those Nisei boys have a place in the American heart, now and forever. . . . We cannot allow a single injustice to be done to the Nisei without defeating the purposes for which we fought.[13]

His sister Mary, recently released from a relocation camp, received the award. Her acceptance speech shows that the patriotism of Japanese-Americans remained strong despite their mistreatment:

> In accepting this distinction for my brother I know that he would want me to say that he was only doing his duty as a soldier of our beloved country.[14]

Less is known about the Japanese-Americans who served as interpreters and intelligence officers during the war. (Many of them had to be trained to speak Japanese before they could be of use.) One of them, James Kazato, explained why he joined the war effort:

> I would do anything for the United States, even risk my life. I had children who were United States citizens and I wanted them to be proud of me, so when I was in camp I volunteered to do something to win the war. The government took me as a member of the O.S.S.—the Office

of Secret Service. I'm very proud of the fact
that I did something to win the war for the
United States even though I was a Japanese
subject.[15]

Throughout the war a number of Japanese-
Americans fought a different battle—against the injustice of their confinement. Perhaps the most famous case is that of Mitsuye Endo of Sacramento. A
nisei who could neither read nor write Japanese,
Miss Endo filed a writ of habeas corpus in 1942.
She contended that, as a loyal American citizen, she
had constitutional rights that made her detention
illegal. Her case went all the way to the Supreme
Court which ruled, two years later on December 18,
1944, that she was right.

On the day before the Supreme Court gave its
verdict, the Army, anticipating the outcome, announced that all the relocation camps were to be
closed. The Japanese-Americans were free to go
home.

But official wartime propaganda had done nothing
to help the cause of Japanese-Americans in American Society. Americans were conditioned to hate
the Japanese. Propaganda posters depicted the "Jap"
enemy as an evil, buck-toothed stereotype. News-
reels showed the Japanese as cruel, vicious fighters.
Unfortunately, the propaganda tended to make no
distinction between the Japanese enemy and people
of Japanese descent who lived in America.

And prejudice dies hard. In 1945, as he was pass-
ing through San Francisco on his way home to

Hawaii, Daniel Inouye, now a captain in the 442nd
Regiment, went into a barbershop.

> "What are you?" the barber asked.
> "I am an American," Inouye said.
> "Yeah . . . I know, but I mean who were
> your ancestors? Chinese?"
> "Japanese," said Inouye.
> "Sorry," the barber said. "We don't serve
> Japs here."[16]

Inouye had lost an arm while fighting in Italy,
and his army uniform was decorated with ribbons
for bravery.

# Chapter 10

# The New Freedom

The return of the Japanese-Americans to the West Coast was not a joyous occasion. Many found that their homes and businesses had been ransacked. Insults were hurled at them; incidents of violence erupted from time to time. Over fifty thousand decided to leave the West Coast and settle elsewhere in America. Another five thousand, disgusted, left for Japan.

Nevertheless, the majority decided to stay and endure the hostility in the hope that the climate would improve. Most of them had a difficult time. Daniel Okimoto remembered:

> My family, like most Japanese-American families all over the West Coast, met with its share of animosity from Negroes, Mexicans, and whites. It was perhaps unavoidable, given the almost insane hatred for "Japs" that had been drummed up during the war, to encounter in-

tense hostility right after Japan's surrender. My
brothers and sisters were called names and
chased around at times by school bullies, but
their problems were mild in comparison with
those of Japanese-Americans in other neighborhoods, who often had to band together to
defend themselves against physical assault. To
protect themselves from gang beatings, some
nisei were forced to swear they were Chinese,
not Japanese.[1]

Some Japanese-Americans, like Roy Yano, had a
more pleasant reception.

All that time my landlord, an Italian fellow,
kept my barbershop for me. During the war,
for those three and a half years, he pulled the
shades down and he just waited for me. When
he heard we were able to come back to California I had a letter from him saying, "Well,
Roy, your shop is ready for you to open up so
you gotta come back."
    . . . I would say I was one of the very few
fortunate ones.[2]

And so the Japanese-Americans set about rebuilding their lives. The federal government agreed
to pay compensation for the losses caused by the
evacuation. Few ever got back all that they had lost
—the average settlement was a paltry ten cents for
every dollar lost—but it was something.
    For some the effort of starting again was too
much. One young Japanese-American explained:

I discovered that my father had owned a grocery store before the war and ended up being
a gardener after it and hating it. Before the war
he took mother out once a week to the movies.
Since the war, my mother has only seen one
movie. Before the war my father didn't drink.
But he died two years ago of alcoholism.[3]

But for most the worst was over. As the story of
Japanese-American hardship and heroism came out,
white Americans, sympathetic and not a little
ashamed, began to accept them. White soldiers who
had fought alongside the nisei spoke out against the
shabby treatment the Japanese received. An attempt
by the California legislature to incorporate the
Alien Land Act of 1920 in the state constitution was
defeated by the voters.

Meanwhile, Japanese-American leaders embarked
on a campaign to establish their rights. They had
two main aims: to gain for the issei the right to become U.S. citizens, and to persuade the government
to allow immigration from Japan to be resumed. On
both counts they were successful. The McCarran-
Walter Act of 1952 repealed the 1924 Oriental
Exclusion Act and extended to Japan a token immigration quota. It also eliminated race as a bar to
citizenship.

But what nobody could do was eliminate the per-
sistent racist attitudes of some Americans. Throughout the 1950s, Japanese-Americans continued to
face prejudice and discrimination, especially in Cali-

fornia. Daniel Okimoto recalled his parents' struggle
to buy a house in Pasadena in 1954:

> They found one that roughly fitted their specifi-
> cations, but because the white neighbors made
> it known that Japanese would not be welcomed,
> they were forced to continue the search else-
> where. After further leg work they discovered
> another house that met their needs. But again
> they were thwarted by white neighbors who
> protested vociferously against "Japs" devaluing
> the property in their neighborhood. Again my
> parents accepted the protests and moved on,
> not wanting to provoke undue trouble, as is
> characteristic of many issei couples.[4]

The parents were not alone in their misery. When
Daniel went into his classroom on his first day at
school, he was greeted by cruel laughter from the
other children. The teacher spoke to him:

> "What's your name, young man?"
> "Daniel Okimoto," I replied, almost whis-
> pering.
> "What? Speak up, young man. I can't hear
> you."
> "Daniel Okimoto," I said louder, my voice
> quivering.
> At the sound of my name the whole room
> broke into convulsed laughter again. . . .
> "Hey, kid," said one of the class tough boys.
> "Is that a Chinaman's name or a Jap's name?

Are you a yellow-bellied Chinaman or a sneaky, dirty Jap?"[5]

Fortunately the nisei—and their offspring the sansei —are better able to cope with discrimination than the unassuming issei. They were born and educated in America and are fully aware of their constitutional rights. They lived through the civil rights movement of the 1960s, which fought racist laws and created a consciousness throughout America of the rights of minority groups. As a result, Japanese-Americans are prepared to assert themselves more forcibly than ever before, even when it means going against their parents' wishes. A nisei student explained:

> My parents urged me, unconsciously I am certain, to perpetuate the stereotype of the quiet, polite, unassuming Asian. But survival in American society requires one to speak up vociferously to defend one's rights and gain recognition.[6]

Young Japanese-Americans today are proud of what they are. To them discrimination, no matter how subtle, is unacceptable and they will continue to fight against it. In this, they show a marked difference in attitude from their parents' generation:

> In spite of their internment during the war, my parents feel a sense of gratitude toward the U.S. For them, the "American Dream" has been realized . . . they have enjoyed modest

success in their business, they have earned and
saved enough for their dream home. . . . I am
happy for them, but for me such attainment is
not enough. I feel where real equality is concerned, we still have a long way to go. Unlike
my parents, I don't feel a sense of gratitude
toward the U.S. What we have, we earned. We
made our opportunities when there were none
and capitalized on them.[7]

In other respects, too, the nisei and sansei differ
from the issei. In common with other first- and
second-generation immigrants, they have moved
away from their families' traditions and values, and
often have trouble coming to terms with their "dou-
ble identity." Noriko Oma explained the dilemma:

If I meet Japanese people, they expect me to
behave according to the Japanese value system,
and I do behave that way because otherwise
I'd cause trouble. If I meet older Japanese people, I show them respect because I am younger.
I am very patient, even if they are angry. But
if I meet American people I don't feel I have to
behave in this rigid way. I just say anything I
want.[8]

When the quota restrictions were eliminated in 1965
a new wave of Japanese immigration started. The
new immigrants were generally well-educated and
many had high professional qualifications which
assured them of getting good jobs. Nevertheless, in

common with earlier generations of immigrants, they experienced a culture shock. Akemi Oura, who came in 1968 when she was twenty-five, explained:

> When we first landed in San Francisco I still couldn't imagine I was in the United States. Then we walked into the terminal and there was one young couple just hugging each other, kissing in front of all those people. Then I realized I was in a different country; we never do that in Japan.
>
> In Japan women don't sit together with a man conversing politically or on general things equally. So I found myself with nothing to say socially—I felt inferior. I never felt that way when I was in Japan.[9]

Gradually Akemi Oura came to terms with the different style of life and culture in America and settled down. Her reflections suggest that, for many Japanese-Americans, the struggle for acceptance may be over at last:

> I think Japanese people are very well accepted in this country. Americans have the same goals as the Japanese—good education and professional success. The Issei came and they worked very hard and they acquired money and then sent their children to school. They stressed very strongly an education. That's why there are many Japanese professional people in this country. . . . I love this country and I have been happy living here.[10]

Nobody could pretend that anti-Japanese sentiment has died out altogether in America. There are
still many Americans who consider the Japanese
unassimilable and inferior. But they are declining in
numbers. With tenacity and hard work, Japanese-
Americans have won the respect of millions of
Americans. Today they are scattered throughout the
country and are involved in most occupations. Many
have made outstanding contributions to the United
States in politics, business, science, and the arts.

And yet, to most Americans, Japanese-Americans
are still "foreigners." It may take another generation
or two until they are finally accepted as Americans.
Until that happens, discrimination is bound to
continue.

# FROM THE PHILIPPINES

# Chapter 11

# The Takeover

The story of immigration from the Philippines has its roots in a struggle for independence that was being waged in the late nineteenth century. For over three hundred years the Philippine Islands had been a colony of Spain. Most of the land was owned either by wealthy Spaniards or by the Roman Catholic Church, whose priests were from Spain. The Filipinos, for the most part, lived in extreme poverty. They farmed the land as sharecroppers and were obliged to turn over a large proportion of what they grew to Spanish landlords.

Resentment against Spanish rule came to a head during the 1880s and 1890s. The Filipinos began to agitate for independence and staged several revolts. None of them was successful.

Then, in 1898, war broke out between the United States and Spain. Although the war was mainly concerned with Cuba, the United States sent warships to the Philippines to destroy the Spanish squadron there. The Filipinos, believing the Americans would help them in their struggle for independence, welcomed the American troops and fought alongside them. Overwhelmed, the Spanish agreed to sell the Philippines to the United States for twenty million dollars.

No one asked the Filipinos what they wanted. They expected to be given the independence they craved. They did not get it.

America was keen to expand its territories and its sphere of influence. The Philippines, rich in timber, metals, and other natural resources, were ripe for development by American entrepreneurs. That was the economic argument. But other reasons were given to support the American imperialist policy. The Filipinos, it was claimed, were ignorant savages. Was it not the duty of white Americans to give leadership to these inferior people? President William McKinley justified his decision to annex the Philippines:

> We could not give them back to Spain—that would be cowardly and dishonorable; . . . we could not leave them to themselves—they were unfit for self-government—and they would soon have anarchy and misrule over there worse than Spain's was; and . . . there was nothing left for us to do but to take them all, and to educate the Filipinos, and uplift and civilize and Christianize them.[1]

As soon as the American decision was announced, fighting broke out between Filipino rebels and American soldiers sent to take over the country. The fighting continued for more than two years. It was a bloody, brutal war. Many Americans, horrified at rumors of American atrocities against the Filipinos, called for the withdrawal of U.S. troops. But they were outnumbered by those who believed that the soldiers' activities were justified. This is what the San Francisco *Argonaut* had to say on the matter in 1902:

> Let us all be frank.
> *We do not want the Filipinos.*
> *We want the Philippines.*
> All of our troubles in this annexation matter have been caused by the presence in the Philippine Islands of the Filipinos. . . .
> . . . There are many millions of them there, and it is to be feared that their extinction will be slow. Still, every man who believes in developing the islands must admit that it cannot be done successfully while the Filipinos are there. They are indolent . . . they occupy land which might be utilized to much better advantage by Americans. Therefore the more of them killed, the better.[2]

Eventually, the Americans captured the rebels' leader and the insurrection was crushed. The Filipinos never gave up hope of independence, but another forty-seven years were to pass before they achieved it.

Meanwhile, the Americans set about "educating and uplifting" the Filipinos, whom they commonly referred to as "our little brown brothers." They established democratic forms of local government, introduced a new judiciary system, and bought large tracts of land from the Church which they then sold, on easy payment terms, to the former tenant farmers. Most significantly, perhaps, they built schools, and here the young Filipinos learned about life in the United States.

The first Filipinos to come to America were from the schools. In 1903 a new educational program was started under which promising students were sent to the United States. After spending a few years in America, the students would return home and teach their people about the American way of life. Several hundred students came to America in this way during the early twentieth century. They were generally well-received and most of them did go back to the Philippines, where they played important roles in education, government, and business.

These students were followed, a few years later, by a second group—this time from the laboring classes. When America took over the Philippines in 1899, Filipinos became American subjects. As such, they had the right to live and work in the United States although, in common with other Asians, they were barred from obtaining U.S. citizenship (which would have given them political power and equal protection under the law). During the early years of this century, many Filipino peasants wanted to leave home. Their lives there had been disrupted by years of futile war and rebellion. The Americans had helped many farmers to buy land and equipment, but they could not help everyone, and large numbers of peasants still lived in poverty. One of them was Fortunato Masong, whose life was described by Filipino writer Manuel Buaken:

> Masong was still a *tao,* which is what a poor farmer is called in the Philippines. His house was made only of bamboo and thatch and any strong wind might topple it over. Masong planted sugar cane, corn, rice, and tobacco. He worked his life away in the fields. His life was not much different from the life of the carabao [water buffalo] which pulled the wooden plow in the rice paddies—no tractors, no trucks.[3]

But there was, it seemed, a way of escaping:

> Then Masong met one of the many American steamship and labor agents who were busy all over the Philippines spreading reports of the huge amounts of money that could be earned in Hawaii and America. The agents of the steamship companies were getting laborers for the sugar-cane and pineapple plantations in Hawaii. Masong decided the work could be no harder than what he was doing, and the wages of $2.00 a day were certainly fine. So he enlisted with the throng of labor recruits.[4]

The indefatigable Hawaiian sugar growers, ever on the lookout for a new source of cheap labor, had moved from China and Japan on to the Philippines. The first Filipinos left for Hawaii in 1906. After

1908, when the Gentlemen's Agreement with Japan barred labor immigration from that country, Filipinos were recruited by the thousands. Just as the Japanese had replaced the Chinese, so the Filipinos replaced the Japanese as agricultural workers. Like the Chinese and Japanese, they went there in the hope of making a fortune and then returning home. Some were successful, among them Fortunato Masong:

> It was three months before Benita heard from her husband, but in his letter was a check of $100—his pay for two months. . . .
> Masong had been disciplined by much hard work so he knew the value of money. What he earned he saved, and sent to his wife. . . . In three years Masong saved $3,000, and he decided it was enough.[5]

Having made his fortune, Masong returned home, established a department store, and became a very wealthy man. Shrewd labor recruiters cashed in on his success to attract other Filipinos to the Hawaiian plantations:

> They point him out as a living proof of what can be had by signing a contract to go to Hawaii. . . . With Masong as a bait, the steamship companies and labor agents have recruited thousands of eager young men.[6]

What those eager young men failed to realize was that Masong was an exception.

> So the people are deceived. They see that
> Masong went to Hawaii. Now he is rich. They
> don't give him credit for business ability, for
> self-denying thrift, for his organizing ability.
> They believe only that all who go to Hawaii
> become rich.[7]

Most were destined for disappointment. But they
had little idea of what was in store for them as they
boarded ship in Manila. They'd heard from their
teachers that America was the land of opportunity
and returning immigrants seemed to prove this.

So more and more Filipinos decided to go off to
make their fortunes. The majority went to Hawaii
to work on the plantations, and by 1920 the Filipino
population of Hawaii had reached over twenty-one
thousand, compared with about four thousand on
the West Coast. During the 1920s immigration from
the Philippines increased even more. Some forty-five
thousand Filipinos arrived on the West Coast, about
sixteen thousand of them from Hawaii, while a further influx into Hawaii swelled the Filipino population there to over sixty thousand.

Like the Chinese and Japanese, the early Filipino
immigrants were mostly young, unmarried men. And
like the former, they, too, became the victims of
prejudice and discrimination.

# Chapter 12

# Victims

Filipino immigrants soon discovered that life in America was not all that had been promised. On the Hawaiian plantations they were expected to work ten or more hours daily for little more than two dollars a day. Back in the Philippines this was a princely sum, but in Hawaii, with the higher cost of living, it was barely enough to live on. Manuel Buaken explained:

> In the Philippines a man has little need for so much money. The clan-and-family bonds of our *barrios* [villages] make sure that every man has his daily rice, his rattan hammock to sleep in, his roof over his head and his wife to comfort him. Not so in the camps of Hawaii. These are traps that have enmeshed and destroyed so many of us.[1]

By 1930 about four thousand Filipinos had moved to Alaska to work in the salmon canneries. They fared little better. One of them reported:

116

We all blessed [the] gong when it sounded at noon and at six o'clock in the evening. But everybody cursed it at five o'clock in the morning. For its devilish sound pierced your ears no matter how deep under the covers you buried your head. And when you have stood for eighteen hours in the cold, slimy fish house, you'd wish to God you were out alone on a lonely island.[2]

The hours were bad enough, and the wages were pitiful, but the workers had another grievance:

The previous day we had lodged a complaint with the boss against the Chinese cook. We let it be known that as human beings we could not stand working from six in the morning to twelve at night and be given hard rice and salted salmon for breakfast. We simply could not eat the stuff.[3]

Wherever they went, the Filipinos, who were mostly unskilled, inexperienced, and unable to speak English, were victimized by ruthless employers. Complained one:

We were forced to sign a paper which stated that each of us owed the contractor twenty dollars for bedding and another twenty for luxuries. What those luxuries were I never found out.[4]

Few of those who lived on the West Coast settled in any one place. During the spring and summer they would drift from farm to farm harvesting crops, then in the fall they would move into the cities and take any work they could find—usually as domestic servants or as restaurant and hotel workers.

As their numbers grew, so did the prejudice against them. A third wave of anti-Oriental agitation swept through California during the 1920s and 1930s as racists, flushed by their success in barring Chinese and Japanese immigrants, turned their attention to the Filipinos. Labor unions brought out the old argument that Filipinos were taking jobs away from American workers—an accusation that turned especially sour during the depression of the 1930s. Filipinos were barred from many restaurants, barbershops, and other public places. Many employers refused to take them on, and landlords turned them away. As a result many Filipinos were forced to live in the worst parts of town:

> [We lived] in the red-light district, where pimps and prostitutes were as numerous as the stars in the sky. It was a noisy and tragic street, where suicides and murders were a daily occurrence, but it was the only place in the city where we could find a room. I often wondered if I would be able to survive it, if I would be able to escape from it unscathed.[5]

Nevertheless, most Filipinos tried to make the best of their time in America. They tended to be far more exuberant and outgoing than the Chinese and Japanese. Spanish, and then American, influence in the Philippines had given them a greater ease and familiarity with Western ways. They liked fine clothes, fast cars and gambling, and enjoyed the company of white women. Group ownership of cars and clothes was quite common, for few could afford to buy luxury items individually. But white Americans condemned them for their extravagances, just as they had condemned the Chinese for being frugal. One labor official stated:

> The Filipino never has a dime. . . . His money goes for cards, women, clothes and the like. The Filipino contractor furnishes some of these things. He brings women (white women) into the camp as well as booze and gives each laborer who cares to indulge a ticket. That is he takes it out of wages.[6]

The fact that prostitution flourished in the labor camps and "Little Manilas" brought widespread condemnation. So, too, did the sight of a Filipino out in public with a white woman. American men resented the competition; parents were scandalized. Reported one outraged citizen:

> The Filipinos are . . . a social menace as they will not leave our white girls alone and frequently intermarry. I saw a sight the other day I never expected to see in Washington, D.C. I went to the automobile show and lo and behold . . . along comes a Filipino and a nice-looking white girl. We followed them around to be sure we were not mistaken. . . . I don't know what she saw in him.[7]

For a Filipino to be seen with a white woman was bad enough. For him to marry one was worse. White racists considered it immoral. The Filipino was an inferior being; he had no right to bring a white woman down to his level. Filipino writer Carlos Bulosan described how one young couple was treated:

> One day a Filipino came to Holtville with his American wife and child. It was blazing noon and the child was hungry. The strangers went to a little restaurant and sat down at a table. When they were refused service, they stayed on, hoping for some consideration. But it was no use. Bewildered, they walked outside; suddenly the child began to cry with hunger. The Filipino went back to the restaurant and asked if he could buy a bottle of milk for his child.
>
> "It is only for my baby," he said humbly.
>
> The proprietor came out from behind the counter. "For *your* baby?" he shouted.
>
> "Yes, sir," said the Filipino.
>
> The proprietor pushed him violently outside. "If you say *that* again in my place, I'll bash your head!" he shouted aloud so that he would attract attention. "You goddam brown monkeys have your nerve, marrying our women. Now get out of this town!"[8]

Desperate, the Filipino tried to plead with the white man. But he had gone too far—the proprietor struck him in the face. At this the Filipino lost control.

Crouching like a leopard, he hurled his whole weight upon the white man, knocking him down instantly. He seized a stone the size of his fist and began smashing it into the man's face. Then the white men in the restaurant seized the small Filipino, beating him unconscious with pieces of wood and with their fists.

He lay inert on the road. When two deputy sheriffs came to take him away, he looked tearfully back at his wife and child.[9]

Californians soon took action to prevent Filipinos from marrying white women. An existing state law forbade whites to marry blacks or Mongolians. Correctly interpreted, that meant that Filipinos were included since, as descendants of people from the Malay Peninsula and other countries of Southeast Asia, they too are Mongolians. However, such was the ignorance of legislators about racial classifications that officials were often left to make their own judgments as to the racial origins of Filipinos.

A court case in 1931 led to clarification of the law. A Filipino who had been denied permission to marry a white woman in Los Angeles appealed against the decision. He claimed that the term *Mongolian* did not include Filipinos, and he won his case. Californians acted quickly. In 1933 the state legislature added "members of the Malayan race" to the list of people whom whites could not marry. By 1937 the states of Nevada, Oregon, and Washington had adopted similar legislation.

Reaction against Filipinos reached its peak during the depression years, when widespread unemployment and hardship caused tempers to boil over. Anti-Filipino riots erupted; the worst was at Watsonville, California, in 1930. There, an angry mob, infuriated at seeing Filipinos dancing with white women in their local dance hall, went on the rampage. One Filipino was killed and over fifty injured.

The Filipinos could not rest peacefully. Wherever they went, they had to be on the lookout for trouble. A plantation worker reported:

> I was about to go to bed when I heard unfamiliar noises outside. Quickly I reached for José's hand and whispered to him to dress. José followed me through the back door. . . . We crept on our bellies until we reached a wide field of tall peas, then we began running away from the town. We had not gone far when we saw our bunkhouse burning.[10]

Along with the violence came the call for Filipino exclusion. Racists had succeeded in excluding the Chinese and Japanese. Why not the Filipinos, too? But the Filipinos were different—they were American nationals. As long as the American flag flew over Manila, there was no way of stopping immigration. So, ironically, the racists and labor leaders who had agitated against Filipino immigration, began to support the Filipinos in their quest for Philippine independence. Eventually, in 1934, Congress passed an act declaring the Philippines a commonwealth, to be granted full independence in 1946. As residents of a commonwealth, Filipinos could now be excluded from entering the United States. A quota of fifty Filipino immigrants a year was adopted. This was the smallest quota provided for any country.

Still the exclusionists were not satisfied. They wanted those Filipinos already in America to be deported. Bewildered and hurt, one Filipino asked:

> Where is the heart of America? I am one of many thousands of young men, born under the American flag, raised as loyal, idealistic Americans under your promises of equality for all, and enticed by glowing tales of educational opportunities. Once here we are met by exploiters, shunted into slums, greeted only by gamblers and prostitutes, taught only the worst in your civilization. America came to us with bright-winged promises of liberty, equality, fraternity. What has become of them?[11]

Forcible deportation of the Filipinos in America was out of the question, but President Roosevelt did go so far as to sign a Repatriation Act in 1935. Under this act the government agreed to pay the expenses of anyone who wished to return to the Philippines. Very few took up the offer, however. Most were settled here and decided to stay. They hoped that, in time, all Asians would be looked upon as Americans. Carlos Bulosan wrote:

> We are all Americans that have toiled and suffered and known oppression and defeat, from

the first Indian that offered peace in Manhattan
to the last Filipino pea picker. . . .

All of us, from the first Adams to the last
Filipino, native born or alien, educated or illiterate— *We are America!*[12]

Prejudice against the Filipinos remained strong for
many years. It was not until the time of World War
II that attitudes began to change.

# Chapter 13

# A Significant Minority

In December 1941, immediately after the assault on Pearl Harbor, Japanese troops landed in the Philippines. Filipino and American troops, under the command of General Douglas MacArthur, fought hard to prevent the Japanese from taking Manila, the capital, but they were unsuccessful. As Japanese troops marched into the capital, the Allies fled to the Bataan Peninsula and to Corregidor Island, which lay to the west of Manila. Robin Prising, who lived in Manila, remembered hearing the news that night:

> On Christmas Eve . . . General MacArthur removed his headquarters from Manila to Corregidor. Father snapped off the radio after the broadcast. The following day, however, he switched on the radio again so that we could hear President Roosevelt in a voice resonant with Christmas cheer promising us that "Help is on the way."[1]

But the promised help did not come. MacArthur was ordered to leave the Philippines, and the Allies, vastly outnumbered, fought a last heroic resistance. The next day, said Robin Prising, brought

> the first reports of the defeat of Bataan. Everybody refused to believe them, just as they refused to believe that General MacArthur had escaped to Australia. Japanese propaganda! Who but a fool could believe that the Japanese could defeat the American and Filipino armies?[2]

But it was true. The last defenders of Bataan were forced to surrender. Resistance continued briefly on the island of Corregidor, but then Corregidor fell and Japan occupied the Philippines.

The Filipinos had fought heroically and won the admiration and respect of the Americans—feelings that were strengthened during the dark years of Japanese occupation. Tales trickled out of Filipino freedom fighters who eluded their Japanese conquerors, vanished into the jungle, and conducted guerrilla operations—ambushing enemy patrols, attacking enemy outposts, and sabotaging enemy supply lines.

For three years the Philippines were under Japanese occupation. Then the tide of war turned. General MacArthur, mounting his "island hopping" campaign from Australia to the Philippines, made good his famous promise: "I shall return!" American soldiers landed and were met on the beaches by Filipino freedom fighters. The reconquest of the

Philippines followed. One year later, in 1946, the long-promised independence for the Philippines became a reality.

The admiration of Americans for the Filipino fighting men brought benefits to the Filipinos in the United States. They were granted the right to become citizens. They began to enter professions that had previously been closed to them. Employers began to accept them in areas where, before the war, they would have met with hostility and discrimination. There were no more violent anti-Filipino riots and, although racial prejudice did not die out altogether, life became a lot easier for Filipinos in America.

During the next twenty years there were few new Filipino immigrants. In 1946, at the same time as they were granted independence, the Philippines were given a new immigration quota. Only one hundred Filipinos a year would be allowed to enter the United States. This quota remained in force until 1965, when the new immigration law abolished the quota system based on national-origins.

After that, a major change in the pattern of immigration took place. Filipinos became one of our largest immigrant groups, along with Mexicans and Cubans. By the late 1970s over thirty thousand Filipinos a year were coming to America—up from about twenty-five hundred in 1965. There was also a change in the type of immigrants who came. The new legislation gave preference first to immigrants with relatives in the United States, and second to immigrants with skills for which the United States had a need. As a result, there has been a noticeable rise in the number of immigrant doctors, nurses, engineers, and other professionals.

Thus, unlike earlier immigrants from the Philippines who were, for the most part, poor and illiterate farm workers, the majority of Filipinos who came in the sixties and seventies were well-educated, professionally trained people. But their reasons for coming were, as one immigrant explained, not very different from those of their predecessors:

> Why do they come? They come for more education. For more money. For more security. To be with families already here. Mostly for a chance to make a better life.[3]

Coupled with this hope for a better life was the desire to escape political repression in the Philippines. There, dissatisfaction with the policies of President Ferdinand Marcos during the 1960s led to widespread unrest and revolt. In an effort to silence his critics, Marcos imposed martial law in 1972, and amended the constitution so that he could remain in office indefinitely. Not surprisingly, these measures led to continuing unrest, and drove many Filipinos away from their homeland and to the United States. As one businessman explained:

> People back home watch what goes on here. They saw how you deposed one President and put in another without a drop of blood being shed. Believe me, if the immigration quota was

bigger, you'd see how many more of us would leave.[4]

Economic necessity has been another major force behind the mass exodus of Filipinos. The cost of living in the Philippines is high while salaries, even for highly qualified professional people, are generally low. Observed one business graduate:

> Wages in Manila are barely enough to answer for my family's needs. I must go abroad to better my chances.[5]

And an accountant:

> It is common for middle-class Filipinos to work at two or even three jobs because of the high cost of living in our country. I have paid as much as $7.50 per pound for chicken [there] because food is not in abundance as it is here. . . . In the United States, hard work is rewarded. In the Philippines, it is part of the struggle to survive.[6]

In addition to the political and economic situation, there is another reason for the exodus of professional people from the Philippines—lack of work. Thanks to a major program of public education, the Philippines have been producing more college graduates than they can employ. Many of these have made their way to the United States, along with those who studied for professional careers intending to leave the Philippines once they were qualified.

So among the most recent immigrants from the Philippines are significant numbers of doctors, dentists, nurses, pharmacists, teachers, accountants, engineers, and lawyers. The majority of them have settled on the West Coast and in Hawaii, but some have made their way east and today Chicago and New York both have sizeable Filipino populations.

Many encountered setbacks upon arriving here. Some found that their qualifications were not recognized and that further study was required. As a result, they were obliged for a while to take any job they could find. A Filipino doctor, for example, worked in a restaurant:

> They didn't know I was a doctor. They might not let me have the job if they had known. Too many places had turned me down saying I was "overqualified." Then I went to work as a meat cutter. They thought I was very good at separating the meat from the bone.[7]

For some, finding a job of any sort wasn't easy. Certain employers, it turned out, were still prejudiced, as one Filipino lawyer discovered:

> I tried to get a job at law offices as a researcher or legal clerk. I answered 25 ads in the newspaper, but every time I went out to the interview, they said the job had been filled.[8]

But for the most part, the Filipinos who have arrived in America in recent years have adapted to the life here with relative ease. They have one big advantage over other immigrant groups: Most of them learned to speak English while in school, and most have some knowledge of American ways. As one immigrant put it:

> The Philippines was an American colony for more than 50 years. Billions of dollars were spent in our country teaching us how to act like Americans. We must have learned our lessons well, because most of the immigrant Filipinos are carrying on the spirit of the American way.[9]

Nevertheless, problems still persist in some Filipino communities. Those immigrants who came earlier this century to work on the plantations of Hawaii and California were almost always poorly paid, despite union efforts to improve their lot. As a result, few of them could afford to give their children a good education, so many first-generation Filipino-Americans are now in low-income jobs. And although racial discrimination is not as rampant as it once was, it still exists in some areas.

Added to this, there is a problem unique to the Filipinos. Many of them feel a sense of alienation for, although they are Orientals, they are not recognized as such. As one Filipino explained:

> Japanese and Chinese are at once categorized as oriental, but not so the Filipino. . . . I have been called Vietnamese, Hawaiian, Indian, Chinese, Japanese, Korean, and even Polynesian just to be safe. Only once or twice in my memory can I recall being said to be Filipino.

. . . To put it lightly, I, like other Filipinos, have become "disoriented."

All of this is not to say that I believe my cultural identity has the ultimate importance in my life . . . but the question of recognition as both a Filipino and an oriental is of great significance to me. . . .

To be an outcast in a white society and an outcast among other orientals leaves the Filipino in that never-never land of social obscurity.[10]

Almost certainly, this feeling of "social obscurity" will disappear in time. The Filipinos were one of our largest immigrant groups during the 1970s. And since the new immigrants are mainly professionals, or skilled workers, they are not moving into rural ethnic neighborhoods, as earlier Filipino immigrants did. They are taking their place in cities and suburbs across the country. As Alfred Munez puts it:

The Filipinos in America today constitute a significant minority, small enough to watch, successful enough to take over important positions, and large enough to decide local elections in certain places. The Filipino wanting to be heard cannot ask for a better chance.[11]

# FROM
# VIETNAM

# Chapter 14

# Refugees

In April 1975, after years of fighting and bloodshed, the Vietnam War came to an end. The American-backed South Vietnamese government collapsed, and Saigon, the capital of South Vietnam, was taken by Communist troops from the north. During the final weeks of the war, thousands of refugees struggled to get out of Vietnam. Frightened and bewildered, they fought to get aboard planes and boats that would take them away.

The American evacuation program, which started a few weeks before the fall of Saigon, soon turned into chaos. The plan had been to evacuate those Americans still in Vietnam, along with certain categories of Vietnamese, but, as reporter Alan Dawson pointed out, "the plan was not working":

> The men and women authorized to leave Vietnam were dependents of American citizens and those who held sensitive jobs and whose lives

were clearly in jeopardy in any change of government from the present to Communist. But newsmen covering the daily evacuation flights saw who was leaving and reported that the plan was not working.

The wealthy, many of whom had become wealthy by preying on their countrymen, bought their way out. Many women paid with their bodies.[1]

This report was borne out by an American doctor at the refugee center on Guam, where many of the Vietnamese were first taken:

They were the VIPs, the cream of the crop, all first-class passengers. Some of the women even wore jewels to the physicals.[2]

Bribing officials was one way of getting out. There were others. Many Americans in Saigon quickly married their mistresses so that the Vietnamese women would qualify for evacuation as the wives of American citizens. Some Americans who had no mistresses also got "married." Alan Dawson explained:

Within a week, there were few beautiful prostitutes in Saigon. Young Americans made the rounds of virtually every bar and whorehouse in the capital to round up the women and sponsor them out of the country. One man claimed he made four trips in and out of Saigon, each time leaving with another "wife" and several "sisters-in-law."[3]

But for most of the Vietnamese who wanted to be evacuated to America, legitimately or otherwise, it was a matter of waiting and hoping:

> Huge lines formed in front of the U.S. Consulate daily, as thousands of Vietnamese asked, begged, pleaded for a way out of the country. Many clutched identification cards showing that they had worked or worked now for the American government.[4]

Those Vietnamese who worked for the American government were on the priority list for evacuation. So, too, were employees of American companies in Vietnam, members of the South Vietnamese government, military leaders, provincial leaders—anybody whose life might be in danger under the new government. During the final days of the evacuation, the Americans worked feverishly to process applications and get these people out of the country.

What they hadn't bargained for, however, was the sheer panic on the part of the ordinary Vietnamese people. Rumors that there would be a bloodbath if the Communists took power ran rife. Indeed, American propagandists had been spreading such rumors for years in their effort to gain the active support of the South Vietnamese in the fight against the Communists. In the panic of the final weeks before the fall of Saigon, the rumors multiplied and were believed. One woman who managed to escape explained:

I would not leave the country and my mother if they did not tell me the dirty stories about the communists. They said that they are going to give each single girl a huge sack containing a sick or handicapped communist soldier to take care of him, and to marry him, or if the men soldiers "need," the single girls have to give. The children born will belong to the government. I rather die than doing these things.[5]

Thousands of people whom the Americans had not planned to evacuate begged to be taken away. Some were lucky. Among the Americans who were controlling the evacuation were some, like this one, who just wanted to help as many people as possible. One described the situation as follows:

I would say that, for those of us that were controlling things . . . you had two basic types: you had the pure bureaucrat who wanted to do everything by the letter and then you had a little more humanitarian people who would try to get some insight into the person [applying for evacuation] and then help him to get out if he had a legitimate reason to go. . . . I think . . . most people felt that there would be some kind of bloodbath once the Communists took over. And for that reason, I myself and a few of my friends were willing to help the most people out that we could.[6]

As Communist troops moved nearer to Saigon, buses were organized to take prearranged groups of

Americans to the Saigon airport for evacuation. Some Vietnamese managed to get out on these. Reporter Alan Dawson explained how they did it:

> There were perhaps 100,000 fairly desperate souls in Saigon, trying to get out of the country before the Communists came in. . . .
> These unfortunate people roamed the streets watching for the first signs of evacuation. Most had the bus stops firmly embedded in their memories. Others just watched for crowds of Americans with shoulder bags. They pleaded, cried and shoved to get aboard the buses. . . . Some few American evacuees felt sorry enough for the Vietnamese to allow them onto the buses ahead of themselves.[7]

Many of the Vietnamese whom the American government had decided not to evacuate found other ways of leaving the country. Those who had small boats took passengers out to sea, for a price, to be picked up by American vessels. Some individuals, including deserters from the South Vietnamese army, commandeered boats at gunpoint. Vietnamese air force pilots loaded their planes with friends, family, and any strangers who could pay the high price demanded, and flew them to American bases in Thailand. Vietnamese navy ships evacuated families and friends of crew members.

On April 28, Communist troops reached the outskirts of Saigon and bombed the Saigon airport. No more evacuation flights could take off from there. On the following day the American ambassador ordered the final evacuation, by helicopter, from the U.S. Embassy in Saigon. Swarms of Vietnamese descended upon the embassy hoping for a last chance to get away. It was a horrifying scene. Fighting crowds had to be forced back with tear gas so that the helicopters could take off. The final flight left shortly after midnight, leaving hundreds of people in the embassy grounds, and on the next day the South Vietnamese government surrendered to the Communists.

The anticipated bloodbath did not take place. During the weeks following the fall of Saigon, the new Communist government set about introducing a new order. Alan Dawson, who stayed on in Saigon, described what happened:

> The capitalist city was finding out what social- ism and communism were all about in the four months I was there, and the huge middle class of Saigon discovered they didn't like it much. Fixed minimum bank withdrawals—when the bank finally opened—of $50 a month per family member was railed against. Registration of gold and jewelry was fought and if possible avoided. The idea of ration cards for daily necessities was unthinkable. But to be fought at all costs was the "redistribution of popula- tion" from overcrowded, unemployed Saigon.[8]

Few Saigon residents wished to leave their city to work in the countryside but, as it turned out, they had little choice. Explained Dawson:

Two forms of coercion were most often employed. In one case, ex-soldiers and officers of the Saigon armed forces had it made clear to them during "reeducation courses" that in order to regain their rights as citizens of Vietnam, they were expected to contribute to the rebuilding of the nation by moving out of Saigon to take up farming.[9]

The second form of coercion, directed at the poorer people, gave them the choice of moving or starving:

[Communist officials] gave rice handouts to the poor once. The second time they were asked for charity, the officials showed up with propagandists—most often students—who gave [the poor] rice together with a lecture on how everyone must work and the place to find work was in the countryside. By the third or fourth visit, officials refused to give rice until the head of the family involved volunteered to leave Saigon with his or her family by the next available transportation.[10]

In this way hundreds of thousands of people were more or less forced to leave Saigon for the countryside. There, under the strict supervision of Communist officials, they worked in the fields, built villages, and tried to adapt to a new life.

For some the effort was too much. People who had worked as clerks, secretaries, bankers, or business executives in the city could not always come to terms with a peasant's existence. They were neither physically nor mentally suited for such a life, but if they showed any signs of resistance, they risked spending months in a "reeducation center"—one of a number of centers set up by the Communists to teach people to understand the new policies in Vietnam.

As a result, thousands of Vietnamese chose to leave Vietnam, even though it meant risking their lives. Unable to take flights out of their country after 1975, they resorted to boats. Every kind of vessel, ranging from small fishing boats to large cargo vessels, was used to ferry the refugees away from Vietnam. For many, the journey by sea was the beginning of a new nightmare.

# Chapter 15

# Resettlement

The first Vietnamese refugees to reach the United States were, for the most part, well-educated, relatively wealthy, and able to speak English. These were the people whom the Americans had planned to bring out—military officers, professional people who had worked for American companies, people who had relatives in the United States. Americans who had feared an influx of poverty-stricken, uneducated refugees felt reassured: These people would have no problems fitting into American life.

But then the pattern changed. Ships arriving in Guam, an American island in the Pacific, carried a different type of refugee:

> Down the gangplanks of the first rescue ships to reach Guam filed thousands of refugees who had fled the Vietnamese coast in small boats—barefoot, poor and bandy-legged, bringing little more with them than the soiled, flimsy clothing they wore, carrying infants and small bundles

143

of belongings. They were not the endangered
elite of a fallen nation, but instead plain
soldiers, fishermen and gnarled farmers.[1]

By mid-May 1975 over 117,000 Vietnamese
refugees had entered United States territory, and
more were on their way. It was clear that resettling
them would be far more difficult than the American
government had anticipated. Finding jobs and homes
for tens of thousands of unskilled people, many of
whom spoke no English, was not going to be easy.
And to make matters worse, the refugees came at a
time when the United States was going through its
worst economic recession since the 1930s. Unemployment was high and many thousands were on
welfare.

Some of the refugees were easier to deal with than
others. Those with relatives in the United States,
often the wives of American servicemen who had
served in Vietnam, were generally taken care of by
their families. Many of those who had worked for
American companies in Vietnam were found housing
and jobs by their former employers.

But this wasn't always the case. Some companies
had made no plans for their Vietnamese employees
and were thrown into confusion. One executive from
Exxon Corporation, which had employed about
seven hundred Vietnamese in its South Vietnam sub-
sidiary, said:

> We don't know who got out, who the hell they
> are or where the hell they are or exactly what
> the hell we are going to do.[2]

Other companies simply had no desire to help their former employees. One official from a multinational concern told a reporter:

> I'm supposed to tell you that we're "trying our best to provide employment assistance." What that means is we're doing as little as we can.[3]

The majority of refugees were taken to reception centers that had been set up on Guam and at three military bases in the United States. There they were interviewed, examined, and provided with temporary accommodations while organizers conducted security checks and then tried to find sponsors for them.

Each Vietnamese family, it had been decided, must have a sponsor—a person, a group of people, or an organization—who would assume responsibility for it. The sponsor would help the head of the household find a job, enroll the children in school, and generally help the family to get along until it was self-supporting.

The task of finding sponsors was handled by a number of volunteer agencies. They got in touch with individual people, clubs, churches, and other organizations and encouraged them to sponsor a family. The response was often disappointing. Many Americans resented the presence of so many Vietnamese. There were not enough jobs to go around, they claimed. The refugees would end up on welfare; why should America take responsibility for them? Why not send them back home?

President Gerald R. Ford was furious at this response. At one meeting he said:

It just burns me up. These great humanitarians
—they just want to turn their backs. We didn't
do it with the Hungarians. We didn't do it with
the Cubans. And damn it, we're not going to
do it now.[4]

And at a press conference:

I am primarily very upset because the United
States has had a long tradition of opening its
doors to immigrants from all countries. . . .
    I understand the attitude of some. We have
serious economic problems. But out of the
120,000 refugees who are either here or on
their way, 60 per cent of those are children.
They ought to be given an opportunity . . .
despite our economic problems I am convinced
that the vast majority of Americans today want
these people to have another opportunity to
escape the probability of death.[5]

But the American people, it seemed, were not convinced. By the beginning of June 1975, only 24,000
of the total of over 130,000 refugees had been
moved out of the reception camps. Some had to wait
several months before sponsors were found for them.
    Matters were complicated by the fact that some
refugees turned down offers of sponsorship, particularly when the sponsors lived in small communities. The Vietnamese were afraid of being
isolated, away from their fellow countrymen, and
preferred to remain in the camps. Another difficulty

arose from the fact that many of the Vietnamese were members of large extended families with eight or more members. It was hard to find sponsors who would take responsibility for large families; offers which involved splitting up the family were consistently turned down.

By October the camp organizers were getting desperate. They had originally expected that all the refugees would be "processed" within three months. They could not afford to feed and house them indefinitely. They decided to be firmer with the remaining refugees. The Vietnamese newspaper in one camp carried this message:

> Camp authorities, given the responsibility of placing thousands of refugees into those American communities, cannot allow the final refugee-sponsor match-up to be changed lightly. The decision has recently been made, therefore, that any refugee rejecting a sponsor must appear before the camp's sponsorship review board to show sufficient cause for the rejection.[6]

After this the process of resettling the Vietnamese speeded up considerably and just before Christmas the last refugee camp closed down. Over 130,000 Vietnamese had been scattered across the United States. The American authorities felt pleased. The sponsorship system meant that there were no large Vietnamese communities; there would be no repetition of the problems associated with Chinatowns and Little Tokyos. Living in communities across the nation, the Vietnamese would soon learn to adapt to American life.

In practice it was a different matter. Many of the Vietnamese had, and continue to have, a very hard time adjusting to their new life. For the thousands who speak little or no English, it has been particularly difficult. Their inability to communicate has often forced them to accept low-paying and menial jobs which in no way reflect their intelligence or work experience. A report in *Time* magazine in 1976 stated:

> Many now work as filling-station attendants, messengers or office clerks. Tran Dinh Chi was once principal of a Saigon high school; now he earns $2.40 an hour as a part-time maintenance man in Michigan. Nguyen An Minh, formerly vice president of a commercial bank, is unemployed in New Orleans largely because he speaks no English. An ex-general is serving as headwaiter at a Pennsylvania restaurant.[7]

Many of the refugees were doctors. In order to practice in the United States they have to pass tests in which they must demonstrate their command of English and knowledge of medicine—no easy task, given their background. Another article in *Time* magazine explained the problem:

> Often fluent in French, many of the refugee physicians speak little English. Nor are they familiar with American medical practice. Viet-

namese medical training, which borrows
heavily from the French, is based more on
books than on clinical experience. Medical
problems are also different. For example,
Vietnamese physicians are used to dealing with
infectious diseases like malaria and tuberculosis
and illnesses caused by parasites. In the U.S.
they will deal with heart disease, strokes and
cancer.[8]

In many areas special classes were set up to teach
English to the Vietnamese refugees. Most of the
students were keen to learn, but they had problems
in mastering the language, as one teacher recalled:

Multisyllabic words . . . are virtually unknown
in Vietnamese. When I drew a picture of a
rhinoceros and a hippopotamus, the class
grinned and recognized the animals immediately. When I told them the names, they
almost wept. We compromised on *rhino* and
*hippo*.[9]

The language barrier, the teacher said, was just one
of many obstacles to be overcome. Many of the
refugees suffered from "culture shock." It was no
simple matter to move from a rural nation to a fast-
food, fast-car industrialized country like the United
States.

In the end, it was the culture shock, rather than
the educational problems, that caused most of
the misery for my students. American manners
and mores, as construed by the Vietnamese

kids and their parents, were not only inscrutable but obnoxious. . . .

The kids made a few friends, but, as a rule, they were with kids from families of recent immigrants from India and Japan who shared some of their old world conservatism.[10]

For some, the effort of trying to adapt was just too much. The teacher recalled the unhappiness of one of his pupils, a former colonel in the South Vietnamese army:

> The lack of Vietnamese to socialize with became unbearable for the Colonel and his wife, and for the kids as their attempts to become "American" failed. After a year, they moved to an enclave of Vietnamese in California, despite the fact that jobs were said to be impossible to find there.
>
> "We have a saying in our country," the Colonel said sadly, . . . "the lake may be small and dirty, but it's our own lake. I don't want to live with Americans."[11]

Many others felt the same way. Vietnamese across the country began to pack up and move to areas where they could enjoy the company of their own people. Families that had been split up got back together again. Entire villages regrouped themselves. Vietnamese associations were formed to provide social, recreational, and educational services.

A large proportion of the Vietnamese moved to California, historically the home of the majority of

Asians in America. Other sizeable communities formed in New Orleans, New York, Dallas, and Chicago. The problems that the American government had hoped to avoid by scattering the refugees across the country began to materialize.

From the start, many Americans had resented the presence of the Vietnamese on their own soil. The refugees were an embarrassing reminder of a frustrating war which had divided this country and in which thousands of Americans had died. Now, as they formed their own communities and became more visible, other resentments built up.

Desperate to earn a living, the Vietnamese accepted low-paying menial jobs. This gave rise to the familiar complaint that they were taking jobs away from Americans. Many Vietnamese were unable to find work at all—by mid-1977 one in three of the refugees was on welfare. Their migration to California, Louisiana, and other areas was, therefore, a cause of great concern. Residents feared that local taxes would have to be raised disproportionately to pay for welfare benefits.

Meanwhile, in refugee camps scattered throughout Southeast Asia were thousands more Vietnamese refugees, many of whom were hoping to come to America. These were the "boat people"—Vietnamese who had preferred to risk their lives at sea rather than to live under the Communist regime. They had sailed in overcrowded fishing boats not meant for the high seas. Many had drowned in storms; many more died from disease or starvation.

For those who survived the boat journey—and

thousands didn't—the major problem was finding
somewhere to land. Refugee camps in Thailand and
Malaysia quickly became overcrowded and the
governments of those countries were unwilling to
accept any more arrivals. Other countries in the
area hoped to avoid the problems associated with a
large refugee population by turning them away.
Cargo ship captains who came across boatloads of
starving refugees were afraid to pick them up for
fear of being unable to unload them. A report in
*U.S. News & World Report* illustrates the problems
of the "floating refugees":

> After rescuing 90 Vietnamese, a Burmese ship
> was forced to wait in Hong Kong harbor for a
> month before docking. An Israeli ship that
> rescued 66 refugees from a sinking vessel was
> denied permission to land them in Hong Kong.
> Later, Israel accepted them as settlers. A
> Japanese ship searched for 64 days for a port
> that would take 31 Vietnamese it had permitted
> to board in the South China Sea. For more than
> four months, a ship with 249 Indo-Chinese
> aboard stood at anchor outside Singapore while
> refugee agencies searched for a nation that
> would take them on.[12]

Unwanted and unwelcome, the refugees could do
nothing but wait aboard their ships or in squalid
refugee camps, and hope that somebody would
accept them. A poet among them described their
situation:

We are the foam floating on the vast ocean.
We are the dust wandering in endless space.
Our cares are lost in the howling wind.[13]

And from a refugee in a camp in Thailand came the lament:

We left Vietnam because life there was not fit for human beings. But life here is not much better. We live like animals. No one wants us. No one cares.[14]

The majority of the boat people who left Vietnam during 1978 and 1979 were ethnic Chinese. Unlike the Vietnamese people, who were not allowed to leave their country, and who had to resort to bribery and subterfuge to get out, the people of Chinese descent were virtually forced to leave.

Vietnam and China were enemies. Many Vietnamese strongly resented the presence of ethnic Chinese in their country, especially after China invaded Vietnam in early 1979. In the months following the invasion many Vietnamese-Chinese were dismissed from their jobs. The Vietnamese government forbade them to work in certain occupations, or to conduct private business. Their children were not allowed to go to school, and it was reported that many Chinese were imprisoned without cause.

The government gave the Chinese a choice: They could either leave the country (and for this "privilege" they had to pay some two thousand dollars) or they would be sent to work in the countryside under conditions of great hardship. Thousands chose to leave. Over 200,000 crossed the border into China, while a further 300,000 put out to sea.

Newspapers across the world reported the plight of the boat people. National governments met to discuss what should be done. The slow process of moving the refugees from the camp to countries that would accept them continued throughout the late 1970s. Nobody knew when it would end. For every family that left the camps to start a new life in another country, there was always another arriving in some dilapidated boat to replace it.

The United States has taken in the largest number of refugees from Vietnam. By the middle of 1979 over 200,000 had arrived here, and thousands more were expected to gain admittance eventually.

Like those who came in the 1975 evacuation, the new refugees have faced the problems of being unable to speak English and of having to accept low-paying menial jobs. But they have had one advantage over their predecessors; they have been able to move into established Vietnamese communities where they can find familiar food, read Vietnamese newspapers, and mix with people whom they understand.

Only time will tell what will become of the Vietnamese in America. They have come to a country that has a long history of prejudice against Asian immigrants, dating back to the mid-nineteenth century. Already there have been signs that history may repeat itself. Residents of a small town in Texas drove out a group of Vietnamese fishermen in 1979 after a dispute over fishing permits. American employers have reportedly been exploiting their Vietnamese workers. Some white neighborhoods have made it clear that they will not welcome Vietnamese residents.

Researchers have found, however, that the 150,000 Vietnamese refugees who have settled in the United States in recent years suffer from psychological distress owing to the general problems of adapting to a new country. Although the Vietnamese have been given free English lessons, job training, and help by a score of agencies, the stress problems have "deep roots in the emotional structure of immigrants and in the nature of resettlement itself that are not so easily reached by a handful of societal programs."[15]

There is also a great difference between the problems of voluntary immigrants and those of evacuated refugees. "It's much harder for the Vietnamese to adapt economically to life here than it was for the influx of Japanese and Chinese immigrants at the turn of the century," says Dr. William Liu, who recently completed a study of Vietnam refugees in Southern California. "It takes the Japanese about three generations to become acculturated in this country. And it's my feeling that it will not be less than a decade before the Vietnamese refugee problems begin to phase out in America."[16]

It would be comforting to think that a supply of goodwill and some sensibly planned programs in education and mental health could help to solve these

problems. Surely a nation which has welcomed so
many millions of immigrants in the past and which
has learned from their problems could find a way
now to reduce the suffering of the most recent newcomers. The Vietnamese, like so many before, will
inevitably end up enriching the life of the country
they've adopted.

# Notes,
# Bibliography,
# A Brief History of U.S. Immigration Laws,
# Index

# Notes

**FROM CHINA**

**Chapter 1.    The Fortune Seekers**

1. Quoted in Russel H. Conwell, *Why and How* (Boston: Lee & Shepard Co., 1871).
2. Ibid.
3. Quoted in Hamilton Holt, ed., *The Life Stories of Undistinguished Americans As Told by Themselves* (New York: James Pott & Co., 1906).
4. Ibid.
5. Ibid.
6. Ibid.

**Chapter 2.    En Route to the Golden Mountain**

1. Quoted in Holt, *Undistinguished Americans.*
2. Albert S. Evans, "From the Orient Direct," *Atlantic Monthly* (November 1869).
3. Ibid.
4. Fong Kum Ngon, *Overland Monthly* (May 1894).
5. Ibid.

6. Quoted in Wayne Moquin, ed., *Makers of America*, Vol. 5 (Chicago: Encyclopaedia Britannica Educational Corp., 1971).
7. Ibid.
8. Ibid.
9. Ibid.

## Chapter 3.    The New Life

1. Quoted in Holt, *Undistinguished Americans*.
2. Quoted in U.S. Senate, *Report of the Joint Special Committee to Investigate Chinese Immigration,* 44th Congress (1877).
3. Ibid.
4. Quoted in Holt, *Undistinguished Americans*.
5. Ibid.
6. Ibid.
7. Ibid.

## Chapter 4.    "The Chinese Must Go!"

1. "Twelve Hundred More," *The Blue and Grey Songster* (San Francisco: S.S. Green, 1877).
2. Quoted in Calvin Lee, *Chinatown, U.S.A.* (New York: Doubleday & Co., 1965).
3. "Despised Races," *Longman's Magazine* (August 1883).
4. Quoted in Lee, *Chinatown, U.S.A.*
5. Ibid.
6. *Why Should the Chinese Go?* (San Francisco: Bruce, 1878).
7. Ibid.
8. Ibid.

9. Holt, *Undistinguished Americans.*

10. Quoted in R.D. McKenzie, *Oriental Exclusion: The Effect of American Immigration Laws, Regulations and Judicial Decisions upon the Chinese and Japanese on the American Pacific Coast* (Chicago: University of Chicago Press, 1928).

11. Fu Chi Hao, "My Reception in America," *The Outlook* (August 1907).


**Chapter 5.   A Continuing Struggle**

1. Interview with Peter Wong in *They Chose America,* Vol. 1 (Princeton: Visual Education Corp., 1975).

2. Ibid.

3. Ibid.

4. Interview with Mary Ching in *They Chose America.*

5. Ibid.

6. Interview with Ken Lee in *They Chose America.*

7. Pardee Lowe, *Father and Glorious Descendant* (Boston: Little, Brown & Company, 1943).

8. Lee, *Chinatown, U.S.A.*

9. Quoted in Amy Tachiki et al., eds., *Roots: An Asian American Reader* (Los Angeles: Continental Graphics, 1971).

10. Ibid.

11. Lowe, *Father and Glorious Descendant.*

12. Lee, *Chinatown, U.S.A.*

13. Quoted in Wayne Moquin, ed., *Makers of America,* Vol. 8 (Chicago: Encyclopaedia Britannica Educational Corp., 1971).

14. Ibid.

15. Laurence Yep, *Child of the Owl* (New York: Dell Publishing Co., 1977).

16. Ibid.

**FROM JAPAN**

**Chapter 6.   Filling the Gap**
1. Quoted anonymously in Holt, *Undistinguished Americans.*
2. Ibid.
3. Ibid.
4. Ibid.
5. Quoted in Ralph S. Kuykendall, *The Hawaiian Kingdom, 1874–1893* (Honolulu: University of Hawaii Press, 1967).
6. (March 22, 1905).
7. Quoted in Tachiki et al., *Roots: An Asian American Reader.*
8. Ibid.

**Chapter 7.   "The Japs Must Go!"**
1. *San Francisco Chronicle* (May 8, 1900).
2. Unpublished interview with Noriko Oma (Princeton: Visual Education Corp.).
3. Emil T.H. Bunje, *The Story of Japanese Farming in California,* WPA Project (Berkeley: University of California, 1937).
4. Quoted in Eliot Grinnell Mears, *Resident Orientals on the American Pacific Coast* (Chicago: University of Chicago Press, 1928).
5. Ibid.
6. Ibid.
7. (November 28, 1921).

**Chapter 8.   The New Yellow Peril**
1. Daniel K. Inouye, *Journey to Washington* (Englewood Cliffs, N.J.: Prentice-Hall, 1967).
2. Ibid.
3. Ibid.

4. Quoted in Arthur A. Hansen and Betty E. Mitson, eds., *Voices Long Silent: an Oral Inquiry into the Japanese American Evacuation* (Fullerton: California State University, Oral History Program, Japanese American Project, 1974.)
5. *San Francisco Examiner* (January 29, 1942).

**Chapter 9.   Prisoners**

1. Interview with Roy Yano in *They Chose America,* Vol. 2.
2. Ibid.
3. Quoted in *Manzanar Community Analysis Report,* No. 36 (July 26, 1943).
4. Interview with Roy Yano in *They Chose America.*
5. Unpublished interview with Hila Shirasowa (Princeton: Visual Education Corp.).
6. Interview with Roy Yano in *They Chose America.*
7. Ibid.
8. Unpublished interview with Hila Shirasowa.
9. Ibid.
10. Daniel K. Okimoto, *American in Disguise* (New York and Tokyo: Walker/Weatherhill, 1971).
11. Ibid.
12. Ibid.
13. Quoted in Bradford Smith, *Americans from Japan* (New York, J.B. Lippincott Company, 1948).
14. *Los Angeles Times* (December 9, 1945).
15. Interview with James Kazato in *They Chose America,* Vol. 2.
16. Allan R. Bosworth, *America's Concentration Camps* (New York: W.W. Norton & Co., 1967).

**Chapter 10.   The New Freedom**

1. Okimoto, *American in Disguise.*
2. Interview with Roy Yano in *They Chose America.*

3. Quoted in Paul Brinkley-Rogers, "Success Story: Outwhiting the Whites," *Newsweek* (June 21, 1971).
4. Okimoto, *American in Disguise.*
5. Ibid.
6. Quoted in Tachiki et al., *Roots: An Asian American Reader.*
7. Ibid.
8. Unpublished interview with Noriko Oma.
9. Interview with Akemi Oura in *They Chose America,* Vol. 2.
10. Ibid.

## FROM THE PHILIPPINES

### Chapter 11.   The Takeover
1. Quoted in Melvin Steinfield, *Cracks in the Melting Pot* (Beverly Hills, Calif.: Glencoe Press, 1973).
2. Ibid.
3. Manuel Buaken, *I Have Lived with the American People* (Caldwell, Idaho: Caxton Printers, 1948).
4. Ibid.
5. Ibid.
6. Ibid.
7. Ibid.

### Chapter 12.   Victims
1. Buaken, *I Have Lived with the American People.*
2. J.C. Dionisio, "A Summer in an Alaskan Cannery," in *Asian-American Authors* (Boston: Houghton Mifflin Company, 1972).
3. Ibid.
4. Carlos Bulosan, *America Is in the Heart* (New York: Harcourt, Brace & Co., 1943).

5. Ibid.
6. Interview by James Woods with Charles F. Crook, Deputy Labor Commissioner, San Joaquin County, Calif., February 1930.
7. Quoted in U.S. House, Committee on Immigration and Naturalization, *Preliminary Hearing Subject to Revising Immigration from Countries of the Western Hemisphere,* 71st Congress (1930).
8. Bulosan, *America Is in the Heart.*
9. Ibid.
10. Ibid.
11. Manuel Buaken, "Where is the Heart of America?" *New Republic* (September 23, 1940).
12. Bulosan, *America Is in the Heart.*


**Chapter 13.  A Significant Minority**
1. Robin Prising, *Manila, Goodbye* (Boston: Houghton Mifflin Company, 1975).
2. Ibid.
3. Michael Sterne, "Manila Strip on Ninth Ave. Is Bit of Home for Filipinos," *The New York Times* (December 30, 1976).
4. Ibid.
5. "Filipinos Throng to Foreign Jobs and Send Their Families Money," *The New York Times* (November 14, 1977).
6. "New Faces: How They're Changing U.S.," *U.S. News & World Report* (February 20, 1978).
7. *Honolulu Advertiser* (November 22, 1971).
8. Earl Caldwell, "Filipinos: A Fast-Growing U.S. Minority," *The New York Times* (March 5, 1971).
9. "New Faces: How They're Changing U.S.," *U.S. News & World Report.*

10. Quoted in Tachiki et al., *Roots: An Asian American Reader*.

11. Alfredo Munez, *The Filipinos in America* (Los Angeles: Mountainview Publishers, 1972).

**FROM VIETNAM**

**Chapter 14.    Refugees**

1. Alan Dawson, *55 Days: The Fall of South Vietnam* (Englewood Cliffs, N.J.: Prentice-Hall, 1977).

2. "Journey to 'Freedom Land,' " *Time* (May 19, 1975).

3. Dawson, *55 Days*.

4. Ibid.

5. Quoted in Gail Paradise Kelly, *From Vietnam to America* (Boulder, Colo.: Westview Press, 1977).

6. Ibid.

7. Dawson, *55 Days*.

8. Ibid.

9. Ibid.

10. Ibid.

**Chapter 15.    Resettlement**

1. "Journey to 'Freedom Land,' " *Time*.

2. "Refugees: Situations Wanted," *Newsweek* (May 19, 1975).

3. Ibid.

4. "A Warmer Welcome for the Homeless," *Time* (May 19, 1975).

5. "We Are a Country Built by Immigrants," *U.S. News & World Report* (May 19, 1975).

6. *Dat Lanh* (October 25, 1975).

7. "Getting a Foot on the Ladder," *Time* (January 5, 1976).

8. "Refugee Medics," *Time* (June 30, 1975).

9. John Koster, "Tutoring Vietnamese Refugees," *Today's Education* (November 1977).

10. Ibid.

11. Ibid.

12. "U.S. Opens Its Doors to the 'Floating Refugees,' " *U.S. News & World Report* (August 15, 1977).

13. Quoted in "Of Many Things," *America* (October 7, 1978).

14. Quoted in "Vietnam's Legacy," *Newsweek* (July 18, 1977).

15. *The New York Times* (September 11, 1979).

16. Ibid.

# Bibliography

**General**

Chin, Frank, et al., eds., *AIIIEEEEE! An Anthology of Asian-American Authors.* Washington, D.C.: Howard University Press, 1974.

Daniels, Roger. *Politics of Prejudice.* Berkeley: University of California Press, 1962.

Hsu, Kai-yu, and Helen Palubinskas, comps. *Asian-American Authors.* Boston: Houghton Mifflin Company, 1972.

Hundley, Norris, ed. *The Asian American: The Historical Experience.* Santa Barbara, Calif.: Clio Books, 1976.

McWilliams, Carey. *Brothers Under the Skin.* Boston: Little, Brown Company, 1964.

Melendy, H. Brett. *Asians in America.* Boston: G.K. Hall & Company, 1977.

————. *The Oriental Americans.* New York: Twayne Publishers, 1972.

Moquin, Wayne, ed. *Makers of America.* Chicago: Encyclopaedia Britannica Educational Corp., 1971.

Steinfield, Melvin. *Cracks in the Melting Pot*. Beverly Hills, Calif.: Glencoe Press, 1973.

Tachiki, Amy, et al., eds. *Roots: An Asian American Reader*. Los Angeles: Continental Graphics, 1971.


**Chinese Immigration**

Chinn, Thomas W., ed. *A History of the Chinese in California*. San Francisco: Chinese Historical Society of America, 1969.

Coolidge, Mary Roberts. *Chinese Immigration*. 1909. Reprint. New York: Arno Press, 1969.

Hahn, Emily. *China Only Yesterday, 1850–1950: A Century of Change*. New York: Doubleday & Co., 1963.

Hsu, Francis L. *The Challenge of the American Dream: The Chinese in the United States*. Belmont, Calif.: Wadsworth Publishing Co., 1971.

Kung, S.S. *Chinese in American Life*. Seattle: University of Washington Press, 1962.

Lee, Calvin. *Chinatown, U.S.A.* New York: Doubleday & Co., 1965.

Lowe, Pardee. *Father and Glorious Descendant*. Boston: Little, Brown & Company, 1943.

McLeod, Alexander. *Pigtails and Gold Dust*. Caldwell, Idaho: Caxton Printers, 1947.

Nee, Victor G., and Brett de Bary Nee. *Long Time Californ': A Documentary Study of an American Chinatown*. New York: Pantheon Books, 1973.

Sung, Betty Lee. *Mountain of Gold*. New York: Macmillan, 1967.

Tung, William L. *The Chinese in America, 1820–1973*. Dobbs Ferry, N.Y.: Oceana Publications, 1974.

Yep, Laurence. *Child of the Owl*. New York: Dell Publishing Co., 1977.

**Japanese Immigration**

Bosworth, Allan R. *America's Concentration Camps.* New York: W.W. Norton & Co., 1967.

Daniels, Roger. *The Politics of Prejudice: The Anti-Japanese Movement in California and the Struggle for Japanese Exclusion.* Berkeley: University of California Press, 1962.

Hosokawa, Bill. *Nisei: The Quiet Americans.* New York: William Morrow & Co., 1969.

Ichihashi, Yamato. *Japanese in the United States: A Critical Study of the Problems of the Japanese Immigrants and Their Children.* 1932. Reprint. New York: Arno Press, 1969.

Kitano, Harry. *Japanese-Americans: The Evolution of a Subculture.* Englewood Cliffs, N.J.: Prentice-Hall, 1969.

Leathers, Noel L. *The Japanese in America.* Minneapolis: Lerner Publications, 1967.

Ogawa, Dennis. *From Japs to Japanese.* Berkeley, Calif.: McCutchan Publishing Co., 1971.

Okimoto, Daniel K. *American in Disguise.* New York and Tokyo: Walker/Weatherhill, 1971.

Smith, Bradford. *Americans from Japan.* New York: J.B. Lippincott Company, 1948.

Sone, Monica. *Nisei Daughter.* Boston: Little, Brown & Company, 1953.

Weglyn, Michi. *Years of Infamy: The Untold Story of America's Concentration Camps.* New York: William Morrow & Co., 1976.


**Filipino Immigration**

Buaken, Manuel. *I Have Lived with the American People.* Caldwell, Idaho: Caxton Printers, 1948.

Bulosan, Carlos. *America Is in the Heart*. New York: Harcourt, Brace & Co., 1943.

Lasker, Bruno. *Filipino Immigration to Continental United States and to Hawaii*. 1931, Reprint. New York: Arno Press, 1969.

Munez, Alfredo. *The Filipinos in America*. Los Angeles: Mountainview Publishers, 1972.

Prising, Robin. *Manila, Goodbye*. Boston: Houghton Mifflin Company, 1975.

Spence, Hartzell. *Marcos of the Philippines*. New York: World Publishing Co., 1969.

Wolff, Leon. *Little Brown Brother*. New York: Doubleday & Co., 1961.

## Vietnamese Immigration

Dawson, Alan. *55 Days: The Fall of South Vietnam*. Englewood Cliffs, N.J.: Prentice-Hall, 1977.

FitzGerald, Frances. *Fire in the Lake*. Boston: Little, Brown & Company, 1972.

Kelly, Gail Paradise. *From Vietnam to America*. Boulder, Colo.: Westview Press, 1977.

Schell, Jonathan. *The Village of Ben Suc*. New York: Alfred A. Knopf, 1967.

Sheehan, Susan. *Ten Vietnamese*. New York: Alfred A. Knopf, 1967.

Sully, Francois. *We the Vietnamese*. New York: Praeger Publishers, 1971.

Thuy, Vuong G. *Getting to Know the Vietnamese and Their Culture*. New York: Frederick Ungar Publishing Co., 1976.

# A Brief History of U.S. Immigration Laws

The authority to formulate immigration policy rests with Congress and is contained in Article 1, Section 8, Clause 3 of the Constitution, which provides that Congress shall have the power to "regulate commerce with foreign nations, and among the several States, and with the Indian tribes."

*Alien Act of 1798:* authorized the deportation of aliens by the President. Expired after two years.

For the next seventy-five years there was no federal legislation restricting admission to, or allowing deportation from, the United States.

*Act of 1875:* excluded criminals and prostitutes and entrusted inspection of immigrants to collectors of the ports.

*Act of 1882:* excluded lunatics and idiots and persons liable to becoming public charges.

First Chinese Exclusion Act.

*Acts of 1885 and 1887:* contract labor laws, which made it unlawful to import aliens under contract for labor or services of any kind. (Exceptions: artists, lecturers, servants, skilled aliens in an industry not yet established in the United States, etc.)

172

*Act of 1888:* amended previous acts to provide for expulsion of aliens landing in violation of contract laws.

*Act of 1891:* first exclusion of persons with certain diseases; felons, also persons having committed crimes involving moral turpitude; polygamists, etc.

*Act of 1903:* further exclusion of persons with certain mental diseases, epilepsy, etc; beggars; also "anarchists or persons who believe in, or advocate the overthrow by force or violence of the Government of the United States or of all government or of all forms of law or the assassination of public officials." Further refined deportation laws.

*Acts of 1907, 1908:* further exclusions for health reasons, such as tuberculosis.

Exclusion of persons detrimental to labor conditions in the United States, specifically Japanese and Korean skilled or unskilled laborers.

Gentlemen's Agreement with Japan: in which Japan agreed to restrictions imposed by the United States.

*Act of 1917:* codified previous exclusion provisions, and added literacy test. Further restricted entry of other Asians.

*Act of 1921:* First Quota Law, in which approximately 350,000 immigrants were permitted entry, mostly from northern or western Europe.

*Act of 1924:* National Origins Quota System set annual limitations on the number of aliens of any nationality immigrating to the U.S. The act also decreed, in a provision aimed primarily at the Japanese, that no alien ineligible for citizenship could be admitted to the U.S.

*"Gigolo Act" of 1937:* allowing deportation of aliens fraudulently marrying in order to enter the United States either by having marriage annulled or by refusing to marry once having entered the country.

*Act of 1940:* Alien Registration Act provided for registration and fingerprinting of all aliens.

*Act of 1943:* Chinese Exclusion Acts repealed.

174        *A Brief History of U.S. Immigration Laws*

*Act of 1945:* War Brides Act admitted during the three years of act's existence approximately 118,000 brides, grooms, and children of servicemen who had married foreign nationals during World War II.

*Act of 1949:* Displaced Persons Act admitted more than four hundred thousand people displaced as a result of World War II (to 1952).

*Act of 1950:* Internal Security Act excluded from immigrating any present or foreign member of the Communist party, and made more easily deportable people of this class already in the U.S. Also provided for alien registration by January 10 of each year.

*Act of 1952:* Immigration and Nationality Act codified all existing legislation; also eliminated race as a bar to immigration.

*Acts of 1953–1956:* Refugee Relief acts admitted orphans, Hungarians after 1956 uprising, skilled sheepherders.

*1957:* special legislation to admit Hungarian refugees.

*1960:* special legislation paroled Cuban refugees into the U.S.

*Act of 1965:* legislation amending act of 1952 phased out national origins quotas by 1968, with new numerical ceilings on a first come, first served basis. Numerical ceilings (per annum): 120,000 for natives of the Western Hemisphere; 170,000 for natives of the Eastern Hemisphere. New preference categories: relatives (74 percent), scientists, artists (10 percent), skilled and unskilled labor (10 percent), refugees (6 percent).

*Act of 1977:* allowed Indo-Chinese who had been paroled into the U.S. to adjust their status to permanent resident.

*1979:* Presidential directive allowed thousands of Vietnamese "boat people" to enter the U.S.

# Index